STAGE
COSTUME

STAGE
COSTUME

MARY T. KIDD

A & C Black • London

A QUARTO BOOK

First published 1996
A & C Black (Publishers) Limited
35 Bedford Row, London WC1R 4JH

© 1996 Quarto Publishing plc

ISBN 0-7136-4445-1

A CIP catalogue record for this book is available from the British Library.

Designed and produced by Quarto Publishing plc
The Old Brewery
6 Blundell Street
London N7 9BH

Editors Maria Morgan, Michelle Pickering
Copy editor Sandy Ransford
Senior art editor Penny Cobb
Designer Hugh Schermuly
Illustrators Terry Evans (Period Costumes)
Elsa Godfrey (Adaptations)
Nicola Gregory (Basic Shapes)
Photographer Chas Wilder
Picture researcher Susannah Jayes
Picture manager Giulia Hetherington
Art director Moira Clinch
Editorial director Mark Dartford

Typeset in the UK by Genesis Typesetting, Laser Quay, Rochester, Kent
Manufactured by Regent Publishing Services Ltd, Hong Kong
Printed by Leefung-Asco Printers Ltd, China

BASIC SHAPES

CONTENTS

PERIOD COSTUMES

INTRODUCTION

STAGE COSTUME contains knowledge gained over many years of making costumes for both the professional and amateur theatre. Its aim is to assist amateur dramatic groups and students of drama in creating beautiful, professional-looking costumes for a wide variety of plays.

Above all, the costumier's primary purpose is to create costumes which help to portray a character to an audience. Recreating historical costumes exactly is neither necessary nor even desirable. The costumier must try to produce costumes which appear authentic on stage but which are also adaptable, hard-wearing and practical to wear – quick changes and ease of movement must be accommodated. Cost, of course, is another factor which can never be forgotten.

STAGE COSTUME has been divided into two sections: Basic Shapes and Period Costumes. The first of these provides step-by-step instructions for making the most basic elements of a costume; the second illustrates how to adapt these basic shapes to produce particular historical styles.

Always budget for accessories. They are essential to many roles and can often be the crowning glory of a costume.

By simplifying costumes into their basic shapes, the less experienced dress-maker will be able to tackle what appear to be quite complex garments which would otherwise be too daunting. All the methods of construction used here have been devised and developed over the years in order to make them as quick and easy to follow as possible and, of course, to

Fabrics and colours must be chosen with great care.

Costumes such as this late medieval dress may appear quite difficult to make but are achieved by adapting a few basic shapes.

produce garments which are appropriate for stage use. It is impossible to show all styles of costume that have been worn through the ages but, by following the examples shown in this book, you will be able to produce costumes which accurately typify certain periods in history. Examples of fabrics, colours, hairstyles and accessories are shown throughout to help you further to reinforce the impression of a particular era.

There are many books about the history of fashion and living conditions throughout the centuries. Study them and you will be able to create variations of your own, using the basic shapes as starting points. Always develop the basic shape of a costume before you tackle the decoration – this is the key to making effective stage costumes.

The chorus line in this production of the musical Brigadoon *can be dressed by adapting existing clothes or by using the basic shapes –* Stage Costume *will show you how.*

Mary. T. Kidd.

Planning and Design

IF YOU ARE RESPONSIBLE FOR

DESIGNING AND MAKING STAGE

COSTUMES YOU WILL BE INVOLVED

IN THE PRODUCTION OF A PLAY

FROM THE VERY FIRST READING OF

THE SCRIPT RIGHT THROUGH

UNTIL THE RUN OF THE PLAY HAS

ENDED AND THE COSTUMES ARE

READY TO BE STORED.

In amateur and student groups the approach to the design and making of costumes differs greatly from that of the professional theatre companies. There is a vast difference in both financial and labour resources. In most amateur groups the money available for costumes is extremely limited, and often there is only one person – usually a dressmaker – responsible for designing and making the costumes. In a professional company a designer liaises with the producer in the design of costumes and set. Costume style is discussed with the producer and director, designs are drawn and approved, and given to the costume department who work closely with the designer in the making of the costumes. A costume department consists of a team of buyers, cutters and costumiers, all of whom are involved in the production of the finished garments.

There are, however, some basic rules that apply to both amateur and professional groups in dressing the play. The first cannot be over-emphasized as it is the key to the production:

EQUIPMENT

SOME AMATEUR DRAMATIC GROUPS MAY BE LUCKY ENOUGH TO HAVE A SEPARATE, WELL EQUIPPED WORKSHOP FOR THE DESIGNERS AND COSTUME MAKERS; OTHERS MAY REQUIRE YOU TO WORK IN YOUR OWN HOME WITH LIMITED RESOURCES. WHATEVER THE CASE CERTAIN ITEMS OF EQUIPMENT ARE ESSENTIAL AND MUST ALWAYS BE TO HAND.

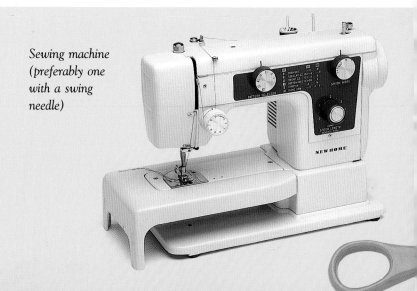

Sewing machine (preferably one with a swing needle)

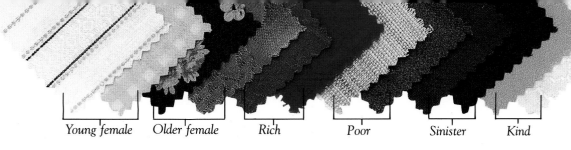

Young female   Older female   Rich   Poor   Sinister   Kind

establish the style and period in which the play is set and do not deviate from it. Costume designers refer to paintings and photographs of the relevant period they wish to depict for accuracy of style and decoration. First, study the variety of silhouettes which period costumes create, such as the exaggerated square of the Tudor man and the rectangular shape made by a Victorian bustle. Concentrate on recreating these basic outlines. Remember that most of the audience will be sitting at a distance from the stage; if the outline is correct, the overall impression of the costumes will be authentic.

Photocopy pictures of costumes in books and shade them in if you are unsure of the shape to aim for.

The second rule is not to dress people out of character. For instance, a courtier should not be dressed in a richer and more elaborate costume than a king, nor a servant more elaborately than a master. Colour and fabric help to establish the character of the role: a sinister character should not be dressed in bright, flamboyant colours – sombre grey or black is more appropriate; young female roles look better wearing lighter shades, older females wearing darker colours. The fabric also helps to create the character. Rough wools, taffetas and cottons denote minor roles and less well-to-do people; velvets and silks signify the lead parts and the aristocracy. Furnishing fabrics are often a better choice than dressmaking ones. There is a greater choice of materials with large, ornamental patterns that quite often provide the richness you require. Furnishing velvets are of a heavier quality and are available in a wider range of colours than dressmaking velvets.

It is a good idea to make a chart listing all of the characters and what costumes and accessories they will need for each act. Many things will quickly become apparent, such as where quick costume changes will be necessary and where a visual imbalance might occur with the colours of the various costumes perhaps contrasting too

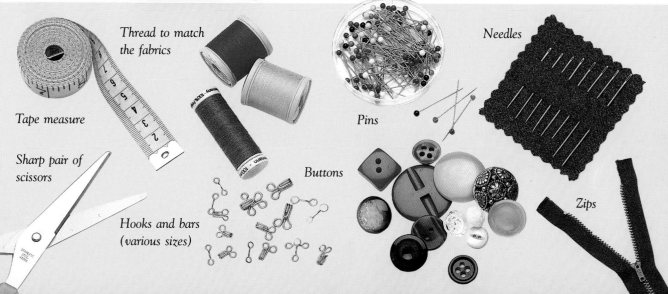

Thread to match the fabrics

Needles

Tape measure

Pins

Sharp pair of scissors

Buttons

Zips

Hooks and bars (various sizes)

much or too little. Once you have planned the look of the play as a whole, you are ready to go into more detail for each costume. Work out a detailed budget, dividing your resources according to the needs of the various characters. Next, make a separate chart for each character, dividing it into sections, one per item of costume. Use this to record colours and fabrics, finished and unfinished costumes, and the budgeted and actual amount spent on each. When you have assembled each part of the costume label it, then tick it off on your chart.

In the meantime, provide rehearsal costumes for the actors to accustom themselves to the type of clothes they will be wearing in the actual production. Use long petticoats as rehearsal skirts for the women. A rectangle of material will suffice as a cloak until the real one is finished. You will also need accessories like hats, fans and parasols for rehearsals; use any old ones that are not part of the actual costume.

MAKING THE COSTUMES

It is easiest for everyone concerned if you take extensive measurements of each actor at the beginning of pre-production. This means that you will be able to get on with costume making even if an actor is unavailable. Make up a standard measurement chart and complete it for each actor. Remember to update the chart regularly. If a costume is to be made from scratch, the next step is to produce patterns. These may

Name _____

dress size _____
bra size _____
suit size _____
shoe size _____
glove size _____
hat size _____
ring size _____
pierced ears _____
left/right handed _____

height _____
neck to waist _____
neck to floor _____
waist to floor _____
waist to crotch _____
underarm to waist _____
inside leg _____

circumference of:
chest _____
waist _____
hips _____
bicep _____

elbow _____
forearm _____
wrist _____
thigh _____

knee _____
calf _____
ankle _____
head _____

nape of neck to shoulder _____
top of shoulder to underarm _____
top of shoulder to elbow _____
top of shoulder to wrist with arm bent _____
inside arm to elbow _____
inside arm to wrist with arm straight _____
elbow to elbow with arms outstretched _____
wrist to wrist with arms outstretched _____

width across front of shoulders _____
width across back of shoulders _____
width across front of chest _____
width across back of chest _____
point to point of chest _____
top of shoulder to point of chest _____

forehead to nape of neck _____
from ear to ear, over top of head _____

[Trace foot on back of chart]

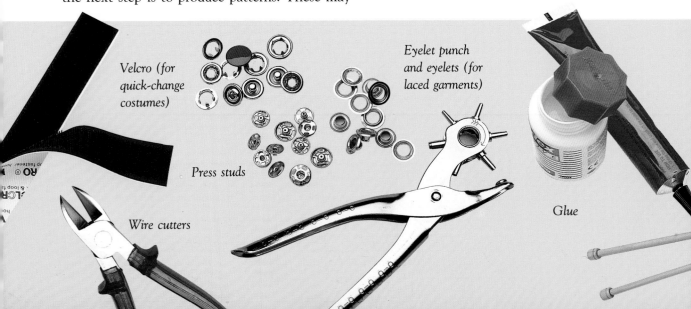

Velcro (for quick-change costumes)

Eyelet punch and eyelets (for laced garments)

Press studs

Wire cutters

Glue

involve cutting up old items of clothing to use as templates, adapting modern ready-made patterns or drawing a paper pattern using the relevant measurements. Each of the costumes in the Basic Shapes section indicates which measurements you will need to make up a pattern for that particular costume. This is called making a block pattern. Always label patterns carefully with the name of the item and the size and store them safely for future use.

Once you are happy with this, calculate the amount of fabric you will need. Throughout the book I have indicated the lengths of fabric needed for costumes but not the width. In most cases I have worked on a 90cm (36in) wide fabric, as for the shirt in the Basic Shapes section, but you can just as easily make it from 120cm (48in) wide material. Some costumes will need adjusting as to the amount of fullness you want; for example, in a skirt you may want more or fewer panels. Work on the principle of allowing extra fabric so you can use it at a later date to change the style of the sleeves, for example, to another period, to save you having to make a new costume. You may also need extra material for running repairs.

If time and money allow, you should next make up at least half the garment in calico to check that the costume design is going to work. This will save precious fabric if drastic changes are necessary. However, regardless of whether you are able to do a test run in calico, always have several fittings with the actor during the course of making the actual costume – these are essential to achieving costumes with a professional-looking fit. If you are adapting existing costumes, plan how the changes can best be achieved and, again, have several fittings to ensure that you get the best possible results.

Time and money will be paramount. Once the date for the dress rehearsal is set you will have to adjust your timetable for finishing the costumes accordingly. Concentrate on finishing the basic shape, leaving decoration and hems to the last. If necessary a hem can be quickly tacked up and decoration glued or tacked on. Whatever happens, don't panic; remain calm throughout. This will inspire confidence in others and ensure greater harmony in the group.

CARING FOR COSTUMES

Keep the costumes looking fresh for each performance. Shirts and cuffs should always be freshly laundered, and the costumes checked after each performance in case they need repairs, and pressed to take out any creases. Bondaweb can help when costumes get torn, though it can only be used if you have time and space at your disposal. For immediate running repairs keep threaded needles and safety pins at the side of the stage. Finally, when the run of the play ends, make all necessary repairs, label the costumes clearly and store them in polythene for use in future productions.

String or yarn and knitting needles (for chain mail)

Brushes (for painting and gluing)

Gold and silver metallic spray paints

Cardboard

Chicken wire

Basic Shapes

BASIC SHAPES  RECTANGLE

A RECTANGLE IS A SIMPLE BUT EXTREMELY VERSATILE SHAPE. IT CAN BECOME ANYTHING FROM A BAGGY PAIR OF TROUSERS TO A FULL-SLEEVED ROMANTIC SHIRT, OR BE USED AS THE BASIS FOR MANY SKIRTS AND CLOAKS.

The actors in this production of Christopher Marlowe's The Jew of Malta *are wearing baggy knee breeches. These are simple to make from wide rectangles of material as they require no shaping.*

SIMPLE TROUSERS

THESE TROUSERS HAVE AN ELASTICATED WAIST AND NO OPENINGS. THEY CAN BE USED FOR STYLES AS VARIED AS THE LEGS OF A PANTOMIME HORSE AND THE SLASHED TROUSERS SEEN IN THE SIXTEENTH AND SEVENTEENTH CENTURIES.

MEASUREMENTS

- waist • hips • inside leg
- from waist to wherever you want the trousers to reach

CUTTING INSTRUCTIONS

- two rectangles to length and width required to go round each leg and hips
- allow for hemming the bottom • allow for a channel at the waist for elastic

ONE

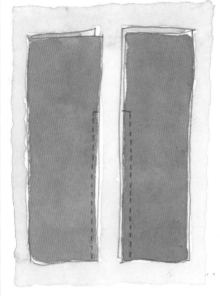

Fold each rectangle in half lengthways with right sides together. Machine each into a leg, leaving open part of the inside seam to form the crotch. The length of the crotch seam is determined by subtracting the inside leg measurement from the overall length.

TWO

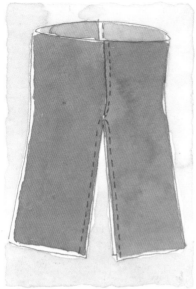

Join the two legs together by the crotch seam. Put the inside leg seams and right sides together, pin in place and then machine the seam.

THREE

Turn down a hem at the waist wide enough to allow an elastic to be threaded through, and machine.

FOUR

Thread elastic through the channel. Sew elastic firmly together to fit the person wearing the trousers, but leave extra elastic inside to enable you to adjust the waist to fit other people.

FIVE

Machine hem the bottom of each leg.

ADAPTING THE BASIC SHAPE

SHAPED CROTCH

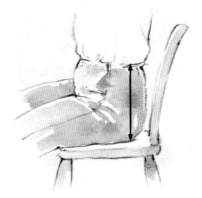

THE SIMPLE PATTERN AND ADAPTATIONS DESCRIBED FORM THE BASIS FOR ALL THE TROUSERS OR BREECHES YOU ARE LIKELY TO NEED. BY MAKING MINOR ADJUSTMENTS YOU CAN ACHIEVE DIFFERENT STYLES FROM TAPERED LEGS TO BAGGY KNEE BREECHES.

KNEE BREECHES

On a pattern the inside leg is shaped at the crotch end to fit better. To establish the depth of the back crotch, sit on a chair and measure from the waist down to the chair, adding 2.5cm (1in) for movement. This gives you the length needed to start the curve in.

USING A PATTERN

If possible buy a ready-made pattern or cut up an old pair of trousers, taking them apart at the seams and copying the basic shape. Use only one leg and discard the other, concentrating on the shape and ignoring pockets and fly openings. If necessary, alter the size before you start, using your measurements.

For baggy knee breaches, cut your rectangles wider where you want the trousers to be baggiest. Run a gathering thread along the hem edge and draw up to width required. Finish off with a band of material cut on the straight. For a tapered style, shape the legs by creating a seam at the folded edge.

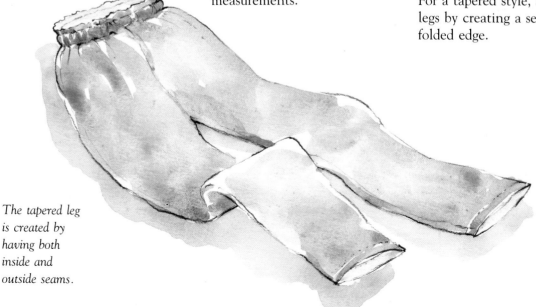

The tapered leg is created by having both inside and outside seams.

FULL-SLEEVED SHIRT

THIS COSTUME IS SO USEFUL YOU WILL FIND YOU CAN NEVER HAVE TOO MANY. THE MEASUREMENTS OF THE WEARER ARE NOT IMPORTANT, UNLESS THEY ARE MUCH SMALLER OR LARGER THAN AVERAGE.

MEASUREMENTS

• no measurements are required for an average sized person • you will need approximately 4m (4yd) of lawn, cotton or taffeta

CUTTING INSTRUCTIONS

• cut a 7.5cm (3in) wide strip of fabric for neck and cuff bindings • cut remainder of fabric into four equal pieces and put two pieces aside for the sleeves and one for the back • cut fourth piece in half to form two front pieces, the selvages becoming the side seams and the raw edges the centre fronts

ONE

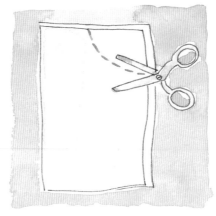

Cut a shallow curve for the neck on each of the front pieces, measuring approximately 10cm (4in) deep and 15cm (6in) wide.

TWO

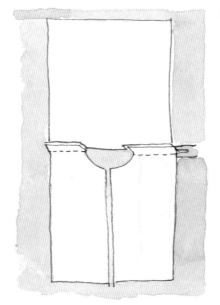

Stitch the back to the fronts as far as the cut-out to make the shoulder seams. While the material is flat, machine a piece of channelling tape along the shoulder seams. Sew one end of a ribbon firmly to the neck edge, then thread it through the channel, allowing enough to tie it to another ribbon attached to the top of the sleeve. The tape and threaded ribbon allow you to adjust the size of the shirt without using gathering threads which often break.

THREE

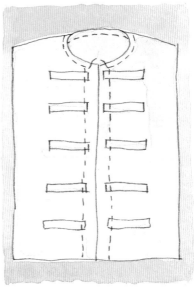

Finish the front edges by turning back 5cm (2in) and making a hem. While machining this, attach tapes for fastenings. Run a gathering thread round the neck opening and draw up to approximately 45cm (18in). Use part of the strip of material to bind the neck. This will also be used as a channel for a ribbon.

FOUR

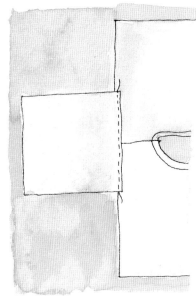

Run a gathering thread along one raw edge of each sleeve, and draw up to approximately 56cm (22in). Centre the sleeve on the shoulder seam, pin it into place and machine.

SIX

At the bottom of each sleeve turn up a small hem and machine. Sew a 1.5cm (⅝in) tape onto the inside of the sleeve about 10cm (4in) up from the hem to form a channel for elastic. Thread elastic through and draw up to 20cm (8in). Sew the ends of the elastic firmly together.

SEVEN

Alternatively, run a gathering thread round the bottom of each sleeve and draw up to 30cm (12in). Bind with a strip of the remaining material. This can be used as a channel for ribbon or elastic. Another option is to turn a hem at the bottom of each sleeve and thread elastic through.

FIVE

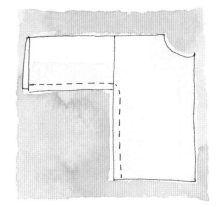

Machine each side seam and sleeve seam in one go.

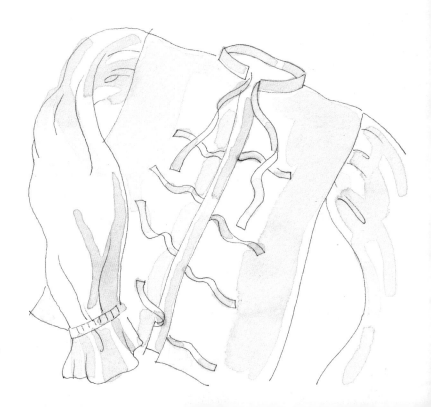

CHITON

THE CHITON IS A BEAUTIFUL, SIMPLE ROBE SUCH AS THOSE WORN BY THE EARLY GREEKS AND ROMANS. THEIR GARMENTS WERE, OF COURSE, MADE BY HAND, AND OFTEN HELD TOGETHER BY ORNATE JEWELLED PINS. THE BASIC CHITON CONSISTS OF ONE LARGE RECTANGLE OF MATERIAL AND INVOLVES NO CUTTING.

MEASUREMENTS

- from elbow to elbow with arms outstretched to establish width of fabric • from back of the neck to the floor to establish length of fabric
- add extra length for the required size of overdrape

CUTTING INSTRUCTIONS

- no cutting is required to make this chiton

ONE

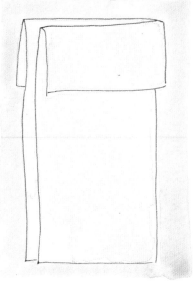

Fold the material in half lengthways to give an opening at one side and a fold at the other side. Fold the material over at one end to give the desired length of overdrape.

TWO

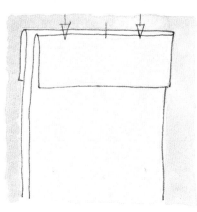

Find the central point of the material at the overdrape end, mark it, and measure equally on either side the width

needed to pass the head through. This will then give you the place for anchoring all four layers of material together.

THREE

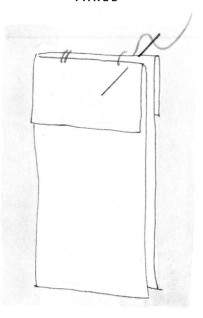

Lay one section on top of the other and sew. The old way would have been to pin the pieces together but it would be more advisable to sew them firmly.

FOUR

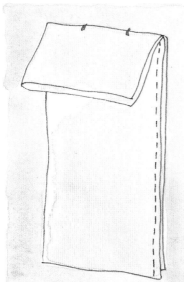

Turn and stitch a hem at the bottom if necessary. For greater propriety you can stitch the open side closed, but only as far as the overdrape.

FIVE

Fit the chiton over the head and one arm of the wearer, slide the other arm through the opening, and use a girdle to tie either round the waist or under the bust.

SKIRT OR PETTICOAT

THIS EXAMPLE IS THE BASIS OF MANY SKIRTS AND PETTICOATS. IT CAN BE MADE FROM TWO OR MORE RECTANGLES OF MATERIAL, DEPENDING ON THE FULLNESS YOU REQUIRE.

MEASUREMENTS

• waist • from waist to wherever you want the skirt to reach

CUTTING INSTRUCTIONS

• measure the length of the skirt along the selvages • cut as many rectangles of this length as you need to achieve the desired fullness

ONE

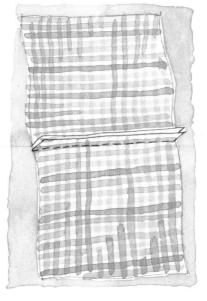

Machine the rectangles of material together at their selvages to make one long strip of fabric.

TWO

Fold and machine a channel at one end to thread an elastic through for the waist. The other end will be the hemline.

THREE

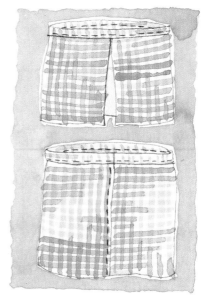

To make an overskirt, neaten the edges but leave the final side seam open. To make a skirt, machine the seam closed.

FOUR

Thread elastic through the waist channel and draw it up to fit, leaving extra elastic inside for adjustment.

FIVE

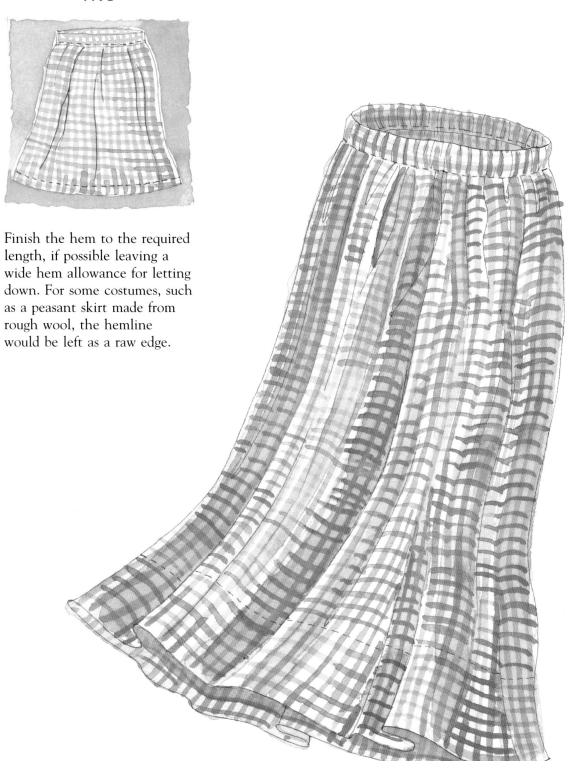

Finish the hem to the required length, if possible leaving a wide hem allowance for letting down. For some costumes, such as a peasant skirt made from rough wool, the hemline would be left as a raw edge.

ADAPTING THE BASIC SHAPE

ONE LAYER

MANY OF THE SKIRTS YOU WILL
NEED FOR PERIOD COSTUMES
ARE MADE FROM RECTANGLES
WHICH ARE THEN ATTACHED TO
A BODICE TO FORM A DRESS.
THEY OFTEN HAVE A
DECORATIVE PANEL OF FABRIC
AT THE FRONT OR ARE MADE AS
TWO LAYERS WITH THE
OVERSKIRT OPENING AT THE
FRONT TO REVEAL A
DECORATIVE UNDERSKIRT.

TRAIN

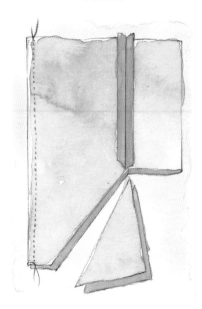

Join two rectangles of the
main fabric of the dress to one
rectangle of the decorative
fabric. Mark the centre of the
front panel and bring the
seams to meet here. Pin the
layers flat like a large pleat
and then use a gathering
thread to draw the waist up to
the desired size.

TWO LAYERS

Making a dress with a separate
under- and overskirt will allow
you to use them for other
costumes. To do this, finish
the waist of the underskirt
with an elastic and the top
skirt with a waistband. Attach
the underskirt to the
waistband of the overskirt at
the centre front only. Attach
the overskirt to the bodice.

To make a skirt with a train
you need one ankle length and
two longer rectangles of
material. Join the three pieces
together and lay the skirt flat
on its side, matching the
seams and lower edges. Use a
straight edge such as a
yardstick to cut from the
shorter front length into the
longer train. Only cut ¾ of the
width of the back skirt. When
you attach it to a bodice to
make a dress, match the side
seams to ensure that most of
the fullness of the skirt is at
the back.

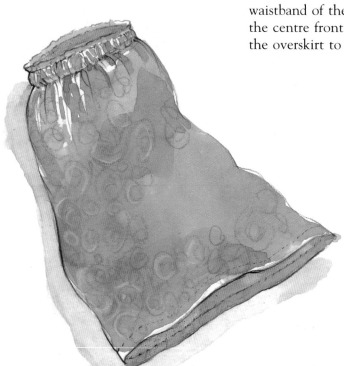

*A lip of material
above the
waistband can
be used to
attach skirts to
bodices.*

Sarong

A SARONG IS SIMPLY A RECTANGLE OF MATERIAL WRAPPED ROUND THE WAIST OR BUST AND TIED ON ITSELF. THE LENGTH AND AMOUNT OF MATERIAL NEEDED WILL VARY ACCORDING TO THE SIZE OF THE WEARER AND THE STYLE YOU WISH TO ACHIEVE.

The simplest way to tie a sarong is at the side of the waist. This allows the skirt to drape at a slight angle. One leg will show when the wearer walks.

The sarong can be crossed over the front of the body and tied behind the neck. Alternatively, it can be tied at the centre front of the bust.

Egyptians wore a garment similar to a sarong. It was a long rectangle of material which was pin tucked at the front or simply tied in a knot. Men would have worn them knee length and women ankle length.

BODICE

Make a short fitted bodice (see page 52), finishing 5cm (2in) above the natural waistline. Allow for an opening at the centre back, extending the material to allow for an overlap for fasteners. Cut and make up a pair of short sleeves, and sew them into the armholes of the bodice.

SARI

A SARI USES A LARGE AMOUNT OF MATERIAL, APPROXIMATELY 6M (6YD). A SHORT FITTED BODICE WITH SHORT SLEEVES, AND A FULL-LENGTH UNDERSKIRT ARE WORN UNDERNEATH THE SARI.

PLEATS

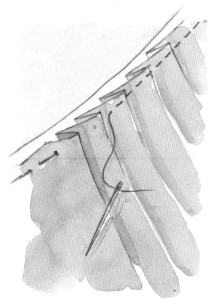

ASSEMBLY

To assemble the outfit first put on the bodice and the underskirt. Then, wrap the sari round the waist and make a number of pleats at the front, on top of one another, like a closed fan. Tuck the top over so it is held in place by the waist of the underskirt.

For stage wear it is useful to tie a tape round the waist and sew the pleats to the tape in order to keep the sari firmly in place.

Leave enough material unpleated to bring up over one shoulder and hang down the back in a long drape. This can also be used to cover the head and shoulders.

CUTTING

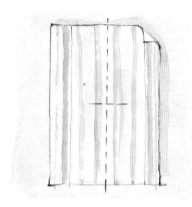

Fold a rectangle or square of material in half and establish the centre point of the fabric to give you the centre mark for the head opening. You can either cut a straight slit across the fabric or make a circle opening wide enough for the head to go through.

PONCHO

A RECTANGLE OF MATERIAL CAN ALSO BE USED TO MAKE A THROW-OVER CAPE OR PONCHO. WORN IN SOUTH AMERICA, AND MADE SIMPLY FROM A BLANKET OR A PIECE OF LEATHER, THE PONCHO IS A VERY PRACTICAL GARMENT. THE WOOLLEN MATERIAL USED IS OFTEN VERY THICK AND WOVEN IN BRIGHT COLOURS, THE EDGES FINISHED BY FRINGING OR WOOLLEN BRAIDS.

A neck opening like that used with the T shape (see page 41) will give a closer fit.

FRINGE

Finish the edges of the poncho with a ready-made woollen fringe or by fringing the material. To sew on a fringe, turn up the edge of the material as if to make a small hem. Lay the fringe over this hem to encase the raw edges and sew into place.

NECK

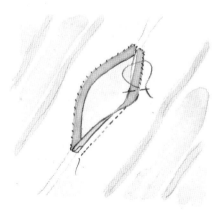

Bind the neck with a flat wool braid, simply encasing the material with the braid and sewing both sides.

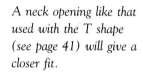

BILLOWING WRAP

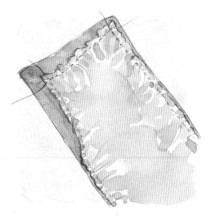

WRAPS

RECTANGLES OF MATERIAL CAN BE USED TO MAKE A VARIETY OF CLOAKS AND WRAPS FOR BOTH OUTDOOR AND INDOOR WEAR. THEY CAN BE MADE AS SEPARATE ITEMS OR ATTACHED TO GARMENTS. WITH A FEW ADAPTATIONS AND BY DRAPING THEM IN DIFFERENT WAYS, A WIDE VARIETY OF STYLES CAN BE ACHIEVED.

SHOULDER TRAIN

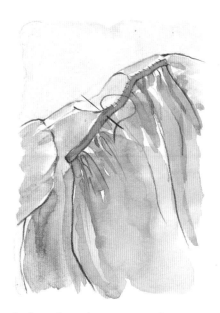

Use a stiff material such as taffeta and cut two rectangles, one larger than the other and in contrasting colours. Use gathering threads to draw up the larger rectangle to the size of the smaller one. Sew in place right sides together, leaving a gap to turn through, and then handstitch this closed. This style of wrap will billow when the wearer moves.

BASIC CLOAK

Use a gathering thread to draw up the neckline edge to the desired size and finish with crossway bind. Neaten all the other edges and attach a clasp at the neck.

A floor-length train can be attached to the back of a dress. Use a gathering thread to draw up the shorter edge of a rectangle to the required width and bind with a crossway strip of fabric. Attach to the shoulder and neck edge of the dress by sewing through the binding. If the dress has a back opening, only sew one shoulder and attach the other shoulder with press studs.

Line the cloak in contrasting fabric for a more dramatic effect.

MATERIALS

You need a stiff band for the base of the ruffs, such as petersham ribbon or curtain heading tape. Organdie ribbon or lace can be used for the pleated section of the ruff, if it is wide enough. If not, use organza to make wider ruffs. Stiffen the ribbon or lace with starch.

RUFFS

RUFFS ARE ESSENTIAL ACCESSORIES IN THE PERIOD STAGE WARDROBE AND WILL ADD THE FINAL TOUCH OF AUTHENTICITY TO MANY COSTUMES. AS DETACHABLE ITEMS, THEY CAN BE USED AGAIN AND AGAIN. SEW TAPES ON THE ENDS TO TIE THEM IN POSITION AND USE PRESS STUDS TO FASTEN THEM CLOSED.

PLEATING

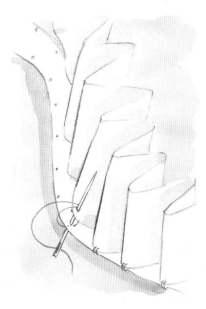

Fold the ruff into accordion pleats and then sew them to the band at the top and bottom, opening them to fit the marks you made on the band. At the open end of the pleats, sew together alternate pleats ¾cm (¼in) in from the edge.

BASEBAND

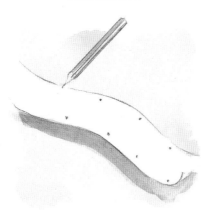

Mark the position of the pleats before sewing. Starting at one end, measure in ¾cm (¼in) along one edge and continue to make ¾cm (¼in) measurements, marking them with a small dot. On the opposite edge of the band and starting at the same end, measure in ¼cm (⅛in) and then ¾cm (¼in) points along the band, marking with a small dot.

If the back part of the ruff needs to stand out, support it with florist's wire sewn onto the folds.

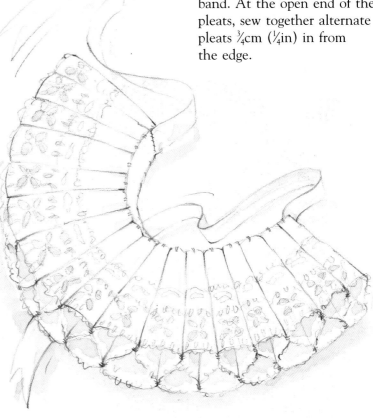

SEMI-CIRCLE

THE SEMI-CIRCLE MAKES ONE OF THE MOST

DRAMATIC AND USEFUL PIECES OF STAGE COSTUME: THE CLOAK. IT IS

ALSO THE BASIS FOR MANY SKIRTS, SUCH AS THE VERY FULL SKIRTS WHICH

BECAME FASHIONABLE DURING THE ROCK 'N' ROLL ERA OF THE 1950s.

*The ecclesiast in Caryl Churchill's Top Girls is easily
recognised by the cape he wears. The colour of the fabric
and the length of the cape help to identify the actor's
character to the audience.*

CLOAK

THIS MAY BE ANYTHING FROM A FULL, FLOWING CLOAK TO THE OVER-CAPE ON MEN'S COATS IN THE LATE EIGHTEENTH AND NINETEENTH CENTURIES.

MEASUREMENTS

- from neck to wherever you want the cloak to reach
- multiply the length by 2 and add ½m (½yd) to establish amount of fabric required

CUTTING INSTRUCTIONS

- cut two 20cm (9in) wide strips of fabric for neck bindings and ties • cut out one semi-circle to length required in both outer and lining fabrics as directed in steps 1–4

ONE

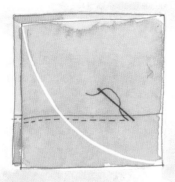

If the cloak you wish to make is too big for the width of your material, add a piece of material at the bottom sweep of the circle. Ignore the join when marking out your semi-circle.

TWO

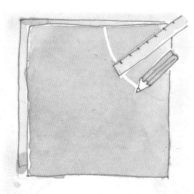

To establish the neckline, fold the material in half, selvage to selvage. Mark out a quarter circle by placing a tape measure on the corner fold and drawing a curve 15cm (6in) in radius.

THREE

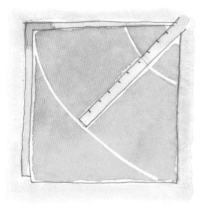

Mark out another quarter circle to establish the hemline. The radius of the curve from the corner fold should be the neck radius plus the length of the cloak you require.

FOUR

Cut out leaving turning allowances of 2cm (¾in) at the neck and hem.

FIVE

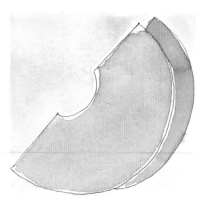

Cut out an identical piece of lining material. Open the fabric out flat and put the lining on top of it, right sides together.

SIX

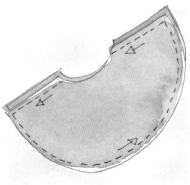

Machine the two pieces of material together, starting at the smaller semi-circle, going down the straight edge and continuing round the larger semi-circle and back along the other straight edge. Don't sew the neck.

SEVEN

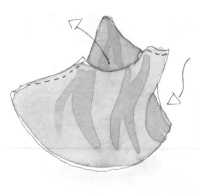

Turn the material through to the right side by feeding it through the opening you have left at the neck (this is called bagging out).

EIGHT

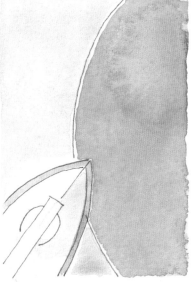

Pull the edges of the seam out flat and press with an iron.

NINE

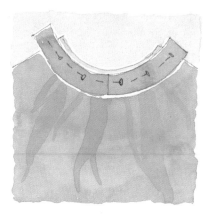

You are now ready to finish the neck edge. Join the two pieces of binding material together. Place the join at the centre of the neck edge on the right side of the cloak. Pin round the neck and machine into place.

TEN

To make the ties, fold the material on to itself to make a tube ending at the neck edge. Machine each tie from the ends up to the neck edge, turn the ties through to the right side and iron flat.

ELEVEN

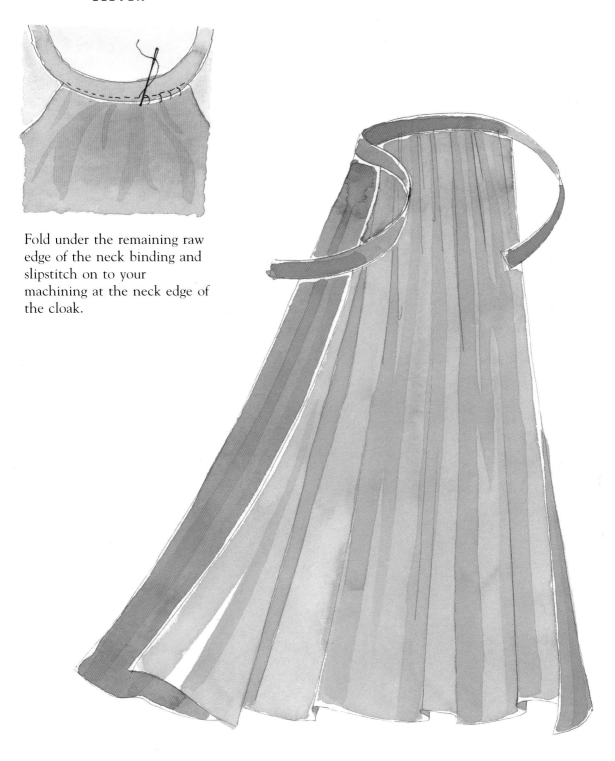

Fold under the remaining raw edge of the neck binding and slipstitch on to your machining at the neck edge of the cloak.

SKIRT

MANY SKIRTS ARE MADE UP BY SEWING TWO HALF CIRCLES TOGETHER. YOU CAN MAKE ONE IN THE SAME WAY AS A CLOAK, THE CUT-OUT FOR THE NECK OF THE CLOAK BECOMING THE WAISTLINE OF THE SKIRT.

MEASUREMENTS

• waist • from waist to wherever you want the skirt to reach • multiply the length by 2 and add ½m (½yd) to establish the amount of fabric required

CUTTING INSTRUCTIONS

• cut an 8cm (3in) wide strip of fabric for waistband
• cut two semi-circles to the length required as directed in step 1

ONE

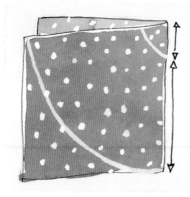

Fold the material in half, selvage to selvage, and cut into two pieces, one for the back and one for the front. Place one on top of the other and fold in half again, selvage to selvage. Divide your waist measurement by four to calculate how wide and deep the first quarter circle must be. Measure a second quarter circle by adding on the length the skirt needs to be.

TWO

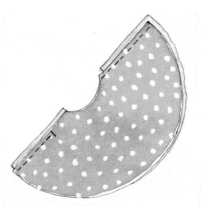

Cut your two half circles, place them right sides together, pin the selvages

together and machine. Leave a 22cm (8½in) opening on one seam at the waist end. Press the seams open and turn through to the right side.

THREE

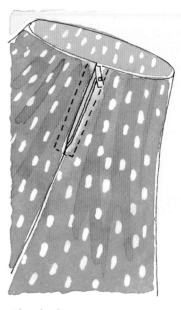

Check the waist measurement. Insert a zip fastener in the opening and stitch in place.

FOUR

Using the strip you cut at the beginning, make a waistband by placing the straight edge of the strip to the circle, right sides together, and machine. Allow a 5cm (2in) overlap at one end for fasteners.

FIVE

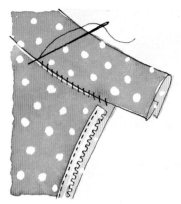

Fold the waistband over the edge of the skirt, turn up a hem, and slipstitch in place.

SIX

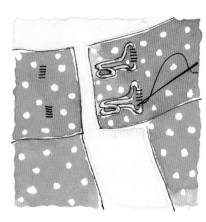

Sew on hooks and bars to fasten the top of the opening.

SEVEN

Turn a hem at the bottom of the skirt and machine or sew into place. With a flare of this type you cannot leave an excess hem allowance as it will not lie flat. A 1.5cm ($\frac{5}{8}$in) finished hem is enough.

PANEL SHAPE

A PANEL SHAPE – THAT IS, A RECTANGLE WHICH NARROWS AT ONE END – CAN BE USED TO MAKE SKIRTS AND SLEEVES. THE SAME TYPE OF PANEL CAN ALSO BE ADAPTED TO CREATE THE BASQUES FOR MEN'S PERIOD COSTUMES.

The costumes in Anton Chekhov's The Three Sisters *are quite plain and severe. The A-line skirts and the sleeves of the jackets are made using the panel shape.*

SLEEVES

FOR SLEEVES THE WIDER END OF THE PANEL SHAPE BECOMES THE ARMHOLE AND THE NARROWER THE CUFF. DRAW STRAIGHT LINES FROM THE TOP WIDTH TO THE BOTTOM TO ESTABLISH YOUR SEAM.

MEASUREMENTS

• from top of shoulder to wrist to establish length of panel • multiply depth of armhole by 2 and add 2.5cm (1in) to establish width of top of panel • width desired at wrist, allowing for hand to pass through

CUTTING INSTRUCTIONS

• cut a pair of sleeves, allowing 1.5cm (⅝in) all round for seams

ONE

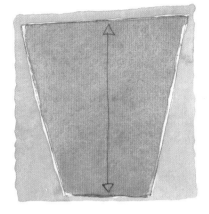

When cutting out the panels remember that the straight grain of the fabric should run along the centre of the panel.

TWO

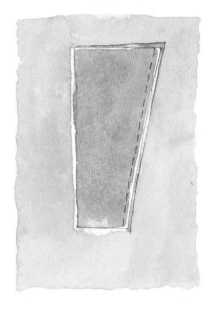

With right sides together, machine the sleeve seams and press them open.

THREE

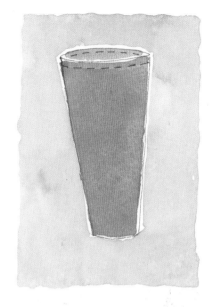

Sew a hem at the top edge. The sleeves are now ready to attach to a doublet or jerkin.

FOUR

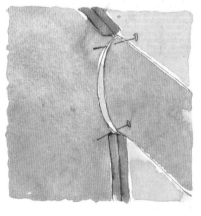

Start by folding the top of each sleeve in half. Pin the centre to the shoulder seam, and the sleeve seam to the side seam of the garment at the armhole edge.

FIVE

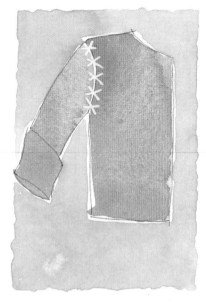

SIX

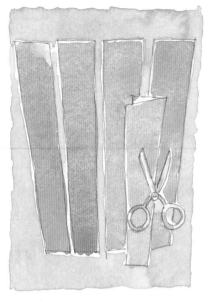

SEVEN

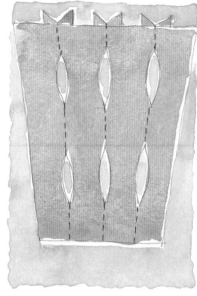

Pin the sleeves in place all the way round. Sew them to the outside of the garment by hand, or lace them to the garment with ties. Finish the cuffs by hemming.

To make slashed sleeves, fold the panel in half lengthways and cut in two. Repeat for however many slashes you require. The panels must be large enough to allow extra material for the seams of the slashes.

Sew the strips together at intervals along their length. Neaten the edges of the openings.

EIGHT

Panel sleeves for period costumes can be shaped at the top (above left) for a better fit. The sleeve seam lies at the front of the arm. A modern panel sleeve (above right) has the seam under the arm.

ADAPTING THE BASIC SHAPE

A-LINE

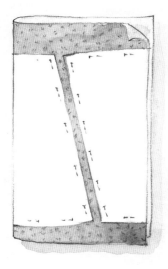

To make a panelled skirt it is often easier to use a pattern for a modern evening skirt. If you are unable to do this you can create a pattern by measurement. Simply divide your waist and desired hem measurement by the number of panels you require.

MEASUREMENTS

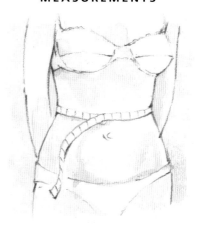

For a six-panelled skirt divide your waist and hem measurements by six. This gives you the top and bottom measurements of each panel.

Flare the skirt from mid-thigh to allow room for movement.

This is an extremely useful skirt and is made from two large panels, one for the front and the other cut into two pieces for the back. Remember that the back panel should be slightly wider to allow for overlaps for a zip.

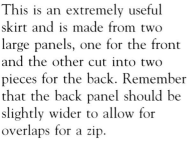

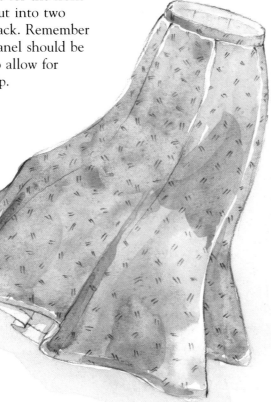

HIP HUGGING

Make the top third of the panel fairly narrow so that it hugs the hips and create an exaggerated flare in the bottom two-thirds. This is done by drawing a curve rather than a straight line for the long edges of the panel.

BASIC SHAPES T SHAPE

THIS SHAPE CAN BE ADAPTED FOR MANY STYLES OF COSTUME, INCLUDING THE TUNICS WORN BY THE ROMANS UNDER THEIR TOGAS. IT IS ALSO THE BASIS OF SOME RELIGIOUS AND NATIONAL COSTUMES, SUCH AS MONKS' HABITS AND JAPANESE KIMONOS.

Shakespeare's Hamlet has been performed in many different theatrical styles throughout the world. Here it is performed by a Japanese kabuki company. The sumptuous costumes are all based on the T shape.

Basic T

The T shape can be made from one piece of material or two, depending on the width of fabric available. It can be cut with or without shoulder seams, or centre back and front seams.

MEASUREMENTS

- chest • hips • depth of armhole • across the back from wrist to wrist with arms outstretched to establish width of fabric required
- centre back from neck to wherever you want it to reach • multiply length by 2 to establish amount of fabric required

CUTTING INSTRUCTIONS

- cut as directed in steps 1–5
- cut sleeves from a separate piece of material if your fabric is not wide enough

ONE

Fold the material in half lengthways and cut it in two. Place the two pieces of material right sides together and pin the selvages together.

TWO

Next fold in half widthways, making four thicknesses of material. The fold of the material will be the shoulder "seam" and the selvages will be the centre back and centre front seams.

THREE

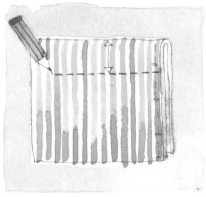

Measure down from the fold the depth required for the armhole, to give you the width of the sleeve. Mark this line across the fabric.

FOUR

Divide the measurement of the chest by four and add 3cm (1¼in) to allow for movement. Measure in from the selvage and mark the measurement at a point level with the lower edge of the sleeve. Mark a straight line down from this point to the raw edge at the bottom. At this stage you can adjust the amount of fullness in the garment, keeping in mind the hip measurement. Cut out from your marks, leaving seam allowances of 1.5cm ($\frac{5}{8}$in).

SIX

FIVE

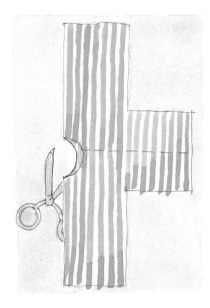

Mark the shoulder fold at the selvage and open the material back into two thicknesses. To make the neck opening measure in 10cm (4in) from the selvage at the fold mark, then measure 3cm (1$\frac{1}{4}$in) up from the fold and 8cm (3in) down from the fold along the selvage. Join the measurements with a curved line and cut out, leaving a turning allowance.

At this stage cut a facing for the neck, using an offcut of material from the side. The facing should be the same shape as the neck, and approximately 8cm (3in) wide. To get the right shape, lay the offcut over the neckline and cut it out.

SEVEN

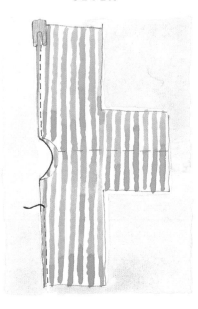

Machine the centre front and back seams, leaving an 18cm (7in) opening from the neck

edge down the front of the garment (the front has the deeper neckline). Press the seams open.

EIGHT

With right sides together, pin the neck facings in place and machine.

NINE

Snip into the seam with scissors to allow it to lie flat when you turn the facing over to bind the neck. Iron the edge flat and slipstitch the facing in place. Neaten the front opening.

TEN

Now fold the material back in half at the shoulders to form the T shape. Pin the sleeve and side seams together, starting from the armpits. Machine these two seams and press them flat.

ELEVEN

Establish the length of the hems, turn them up and sew in place.

ADAPTING THE BASIC SHAPE

WIZARD

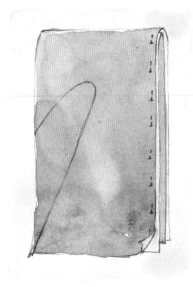

THE T SHAPE FORMS THE BASIS OF MANY COSTUMES. SMALL ALTERATIONS CAN BE MADE AT THE CUTTING STAGE OR SIMPLE ACCESSORIES ADDED WHICH WILL TRANSFORM THIS SIMPLE TUNIC INTO COSTUMES AS DIVERSE AS THAT OF A WIZARD OR A MONK.

MONK

SLEEVES

If your original material is not wide enough, cut the sleeves of the T shape as separate items.

Flare out the skirt of the T shape and extend the lower edge of the arm in a curve to form an exaggerated point which will hang down below the wrist.

All that is required to make a monk's habit is a T shape and a simple overtunic which is made from two rectangles long enough to reach from shoulder to calf and wide enough to stretch from shoulder to shoulder. Cut a semi-circle from each rectangle at one end to form the neck and sew together at the shoulder seams. A large hood made from two rectangles of material can be added to the neck of the T shape if desired.

Curving the underarm seam will strengthen the garment.

The basic T shape can be used for the tunic or a simple variation can be made. Draw a line on your pattern from the outside edge of the top of sleeve right down to the hem. Sew the front and back together at the hem only so that the sides are left open to allow greater freedom of movement.

BUBU AND DANSHIKI

MANY AFRICAN STYLES USE THE T SHAPE. A NIGERIAN DRESS CALLED A *BUBU* IS A T SHAPE THAT NARROWS TOWARDS THE HEM, AND IS OFTEN DECORATED WITH EMBROIDERY DOWN THE FRONT AND ROUND THE BACK OF THE NECK. THE MEN'S EQUIVALENT IS CALLED *DANSHIKI*, AND CONSISTS OF LOOSE DRAWSTRING TROUSERS AND A LOOSE T-SHAPED TOP GARMENT WHICH HANGS TO THE KNEES.

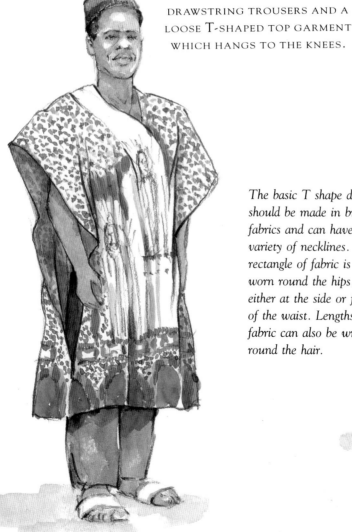

The basic T shape dress should be made in bright fabrics and can have a variety of necklines. A rectangle of fabric is often worn round the hips, tied either at the side or front of the waist. Lengths of fabric can also be wrapped round the hair.

TUNIC

Make the basic T shape in a heavy, buff-coloured drill cotton, keeping the shape of the garment quite straight.

NATIVE AMERICAN

TRADITIONAL NATIVE AMERICAN CLOTHES WERE MADE IN FINE LEATHER AND DECORATED WITH BEADS. THEY HAD FRINGED HEMS, SLEEVES AND SHOULDERS.

HEADDRESS

FRINGE

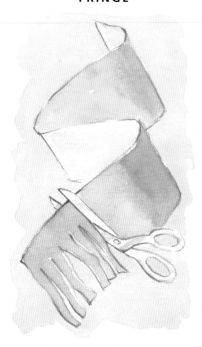

Make the fringe from a synthetic material like suedette in a similar buff colour to the tunic. Cut 10cm (4in) wide strips into a fringe, remembering to cut only one edge and to leave at least 1.5cm (½in) uncut. Use these fringed strips to decorate the tunic and trousers.

Feather headdresses are an important part of this costume. They vary a great deal, so it is best to consult a reference book. A simple headdress can be made from a decorative piece of braid tied round the forehead, with a feather inserted at the back.

Trousers can be made using the rectangle (see page 15), decorating the fold "seams" with fringes.

BINDING

Cut a crossway strip of fabric 10cm (4in) wide and long enough to go right round the neck and front edges. Place the kimono and the strip right sides together and, starting at one hem edge, machine, leaving a seam allowance of 1.5cm (½in). Encase the seam by bringing the material over. Turn in 1.5cm (½in) and hand-sew onto the machining.

KIMONO

A KIMONO CAN BE MADE WITH THE T SHAPE, LEAVING OPEN THE FRONT SEAM. THE BACK OF THE NECK IS AS BEFORE, BUT THE FRONT IS CUT AS A SOFT V SHAPE, FLOWING INTO A STRAIGHT EDGE. INSTEAD OF USING A FACING, ONE CONTINUAL PIECE OF CROSSWAY FABRIC FINISHES THE FRONT EDGE AND NECK.

EXTENDED SLEEVES

OBI AND BELT

For a man, use a simple self-tie belt. For a woman, use a long, wide rectangle of fabric to form an obi which should lie flat at the front and form a large loop at the back.

Cut the sleeve to finish just below the elbow, then cut a rectangle of material wide enough to complete the length of the sleeve and 1.5m (5ft) long. Sew the ends of the rectangle together to form a tube. Divide the tube in half, and place the centre point to the centre of the sleeve. Pin into place and machine, to make a flowing lower sleeve. Leave the extended sleeve open at the back but neaten it by sewing a small hem. Neaten the cuff end.

Make the binding and hanging sleeves from a contrasting fabric.

BODICE

THE BODICE IS AN ESSENTIAL ITEM IN THE
PERIOD COSTUME WARDROBE AND FORMS THE BASIS OF MANY STYLES OF
JACKET, DOUBLET AND DRESS. MEN'S CLOTHES USUALLY HAVE AN
OPENING AT THE FRONT, WOMEN'S AT EITHER BACK OR FRONT.

*The importance of the bodice cannot be overemphasised.
Not only is it used to make dresses and waistcoats, as
shown in this production of Molière's* Tartuffe, *but it
also forms the starting point for jackets and coats.*

LONG BODICE

ADAPT AN EXISTING PATTERN
TO THE SIZE REQUIRED OR
MAKE YOUR OWN.

MEASUREMENTS

• from nape of neck to waist
and then to length required
• from centre front of neck to
waist and then to length
required • width of each
shoulder from nape of neck
• width across back of
shoulders • width across back
of chest • width across front
of chest • chest • from point
to point of chest • waist
• widest part of hips • depth
of armholes • from underarms
to waist • multiply length by
2 to establish amount of
material required

CUTTING
INSTRUCTIONS

• make a paper or cloth block
pattern from the above
measurements • cut as
directed in step 1

ONE

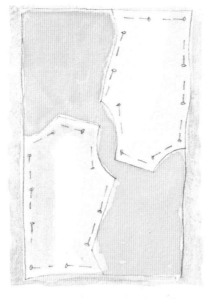

Fold the material lengthways
and lay the block pattern on it
so that the selvage of the
material is where you want the
opening to be. Cut out,
leaving enough material on
the opening edges to act as
facings or overlaps.

TWO

Pin the shoulders right sides
together and machine. Press
the seams open.

THREE

If you didn't make the
neckline shape on your
pattern, do it now. It can be
round, V shaped, square or a
front slit like that of the T
shape (see page 41).

FOUR

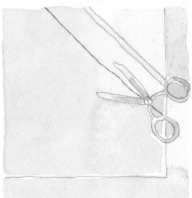

Finish the neck and armholes
with a crossway bind. Cut the
binding strips diagonally across
the material, not along the
straight grain of the fabric.

FIVE

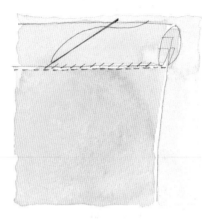

SIX

SEVEN

Place the binding on the right side of the bodice fabric and machine. Turn the binding over to encase the raw edges and slipstitch in place on the machining. Finishing the neck and armholes in this way allows more scope for altering the garment.

Pin the side seams right sides together and machine. Press the seams open.

Turn back the edges of the opening and sew so that they meet. Eyelets can then be punched into the material for lacing together. Alternatively, make an overlap for buttons and buttonholes by extending out from the centre mark by 3cm (1¼in) on both pieces and sew into place. Turn the hem to the required length and sew.

ADAPTING THE BASIC SHAPE

PLEATING

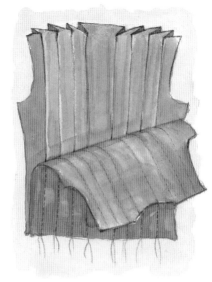

THE LONG FITTED BODICE, EXTENDED TO WHATEVER LENGTH REQUIRED AND WITH PANEL SLEEVES ADDED, FORMS A DOUBLET. A USEFUL VARIATION FOR PERIOD COSTUMES IS TO PAD THE DOUBLET.

SLEEVES

CUTTING

Only the lining material (calico or sheeting) should be cut into the bodice shape. The outer material should be left as wide rectangles, one for the back and two for the fronts. Tack thin layers of wadding to the outer fabric and lay this over the relevant lining pieces.

Pleat the fronts at regular intervals from the front edges towards the armholes, sewing the underfold of each pleat to the inner bodice from shoulder to hem. For the back, start with a central box pleat, and then continue pleating towards the armholes. Only pleat to the armhole edge, leaving the underarm section unpleated. Finally, trim the outer material to the shape of the bodice linings and finish the edges with crossway bind.

Only pleat the central part of the sleeves, starting with a box pleat. The pleats will taper from the shoulder to the cuff. Bind both hems with crossway bind and sew the sleeves to the bodice by butting the two binds together and sewing through them by hand.

Press studs are the easiest form of fasteners.

SEAMS AND DARTS

SHORT BODICE

To make a short bodice take the wearer's measurements as before and make a pattern, but finish it at the waist. Make any alterations in style before cutting, such as seams and darts and a dropped front waist.

POINTED FRONT

Extend your pattern down from the waistline at the centre front for the distance required and mark. Draw lines connecting this mark to the sides of the waistline, gently curving them to create a more attractive shape.

Establish the position of seams or darts by taking the following measurements: from the shoulder to the point of the bust, to under the bust, and to the waist; and across the front of the bust, point to point. The measurement across the front of the bust is a seam line; the under-bust measurement gives the line for creating an empire bodice and the waist measurement gives the line for creating a standard short bodice.

PIPING

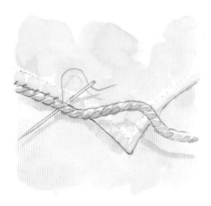

Change the shape of the shoulders on your pattern for a wider neckline.

You may leave the waistline unfinished at this time to attach to a skirt or basque, or you can finish the edge with a piping cord. This can be used as shown but is usually encased in fabric (see page 138).

PEPLUM STYLE

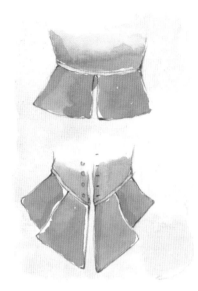

A basque can be cut in several pieces so that it flounces like a peplum. Cut the back in two pieces, straight at the centre but flaring out at the sides. Cut the front in two or four pieces for each side. The centre front can be extended to a point and the pieces can gradually reduce in size towards the side edge if desired. Overlap the pieces if necessary and sew in place.

OPENING EDGE

For a front opening, cut the front panel of the basque about 8cm (3in) wider at the centre than the back panel. Fold it in half lengthways and cut in two. The extra material at the centre forms the overlaps for fasteners.

BASQUE

A BASQUE – THAT IS, A SHORT SKIRT – CAN BE ADDED TO THE SHORT FITTED BODICE TO FORM ANOTHER STYLE OF DOUBLET. THE SKIRT IS MADE FROM THE PANEL SHAPE AND THE STRAIGHT GRAIN OF THE FABRIC SHOULD RUN ALONG THE CENTRE BACK AND CENTRE FRONT EDGES. BASQUES VARY IN SIZE AND SHAPE AND CAN BE STIFFENED, LEFT TO DRAPE LOOSELY, PLEATED OR FLOUNCED LIKE A PEPLUM.

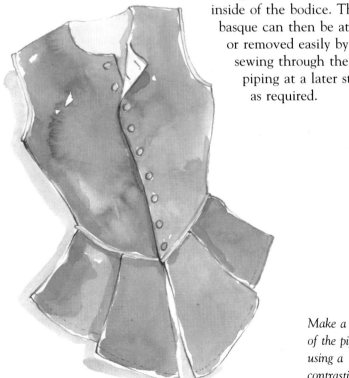

ASSEMBLY

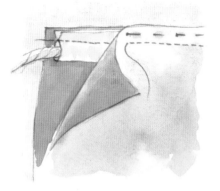

Make the waist measurement and side seams of the basque correspond with those of the bodice and sew directly together or join through a piece of piping, as shown. Alternatively, complete the hem of the bodice with piping, tacking the raw edges to the inside of the bodice. The basque can then be attached or removed easily by sewing through the piping at a later stage, as required.

Make a feature of the piping by using a contrasting colour.

CUTTING

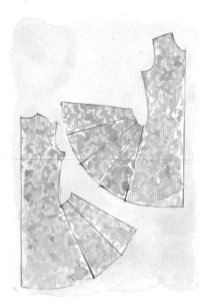

Use the long fitted bodice measurements for the body of the coat, flaring it out at the sides to form pleats. Stiffen the fronts and back skirt pieces with vilene or canvas.

RESTORATION COAT

THIS COAT IS QUITE COMPLICATED TO CUT, BUT IT CAN BE CONSTRUCTED QUITE EASILY USING THE BAGGING OUT METHOD (SEE PAGE 138). YOU SHOULD ALWAYS FIT THE GARMENT ON THE WEARER AT VARIOUS STAGES DURING CONSTRUCTION IN ORDER TO MAKE ANY NECESSARY ADJUSTMENTS.

PLEATING

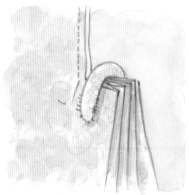

Press the extended skirt into pleats, then sew through the top of the pleats to anchor them together. The pleats should fan out. To ensure that they do not lie flat against the body, sew a small padded U shape over the join of the pleats to hold it in position. You can sew a button at the top of the pleats on the outside of the coat.

SLEEVES

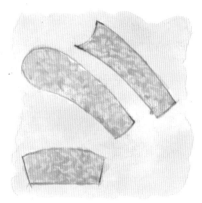

The sleeves are cut in two pieces and separate cuffs should be attached. The cuffs should be wedge-shaped and stand out from the sleeves.

Pocket flaps should be attached.

CUTTING

SWALLOW COAT

THE SWALLOW COAT IS A TAILORED GARMENT AND IS MADE IN A SIMILAR WAY TO SOME MODERN PATTERNS. IT IS QUITE COMPLICATED TO MAKE SO THE SIMPLIFIED BAGGING OUT METHOD (SEE PAGE 138) SHOULD BE USED.

SLEEVES

Use a modern two-piece sleeve pattern and attach separate cuffs which should measure 10cm (4in) when finished.

TAILS

Stiffen the fronts and skirt of the back with vilene or canvas before you begin constructing the garment.

The long fitted bodice forms the body of the coat. There is a centre back seam with an opening from the hem to the crotch. Cut the bottom of the back straight to the side seams. Cut the fronts to fit close to the natural neckline, allowing for turnings at the centre fronts from the waist up for the fastenings. The fronts should curve gently from the waistline to finish at thigh length at the side seams. This curve then continues to the back, leaving the centre part of the back hem straight. The collar is a simple rectangle of material stiffened with vilene or canvas.

Buttons should be attached for decorative purposes but buttonholes are often unnecessary for stage wear.

CUTTING

Finish the bodice of the coat at waist level and cut the fronts so that they finish at the natural neckline. Allow for a fastenings overlap at the centre front, and cut a facing for the front edges to form the revers. An extra 5cm (2in) overlap is required for a double-breasted coat.

BACK TAILS

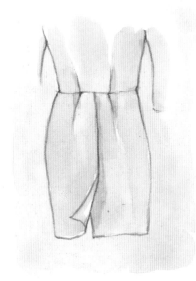

Cut the back tails in a panel shape, and stiffen them and the fronts of the coat with canvas or vilene. The panels should be wide enough at the waist edge so that they can be overlapped by 2.5cm (1in) at the centre back, left over right, and then pleated inwards 10cm (4in) from the centre back on each side.

TAILED COATS

EMPIRE AND FROCK COATS ARE BOTH MADE USING THE SHORT FITTED BODICE AND ATTACHING SEPARATE TAILS/SKIRTS. THE DIFFERENCE BETWEEN THE TWO IS THAT THE FROCK COAT HAS PANEL-SHAPED FRONT SKIRTS AS WELL AS BACK SKIRTS AND IS DOUBLE BREASTED. USE A MODERN TWO-PIECE SLEEVE PATTERN AND A STIFFENED RECTANGLE OF FABRIC FOR THE COLLAR. CONSTRUCT THE COATS USING THE BAGGING OUT METHOD (SEE PAGE 138).

FRONT SKIRTS

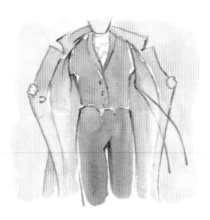

To ensure that a coat with front skirts hangs correctly, sew two long tapes to the left underarm edge on the inside, and a loop on the front edge of the waist of the right front piece to tie them to.

Early tailed coats had slightly puffed sleeves; later they were smoothly fitted.

DOUBLE BREASTED

SKIRT FLAPS

UNIFORMS

MOST UNIFORMS FOLLOW THE STYLE OF THE PERIOD. THE BASIC PATTERNS FOR OPPOSING FORCES, THEREFORE, WILL OFTEN BE VERY SIMILAR AND ONLY REQUIRE A FEW BASIC ADAPTATIONS WITH MOST OF THE DISTINGUISHING FEATURES BEING IN THE FORM OF DECORATION AND COLOUR.

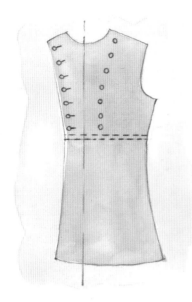

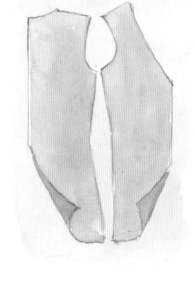

A double-breasted uniform jacket is made by extending both front pieces, as shown. The skirts can be very short, crotch length or knee length and should be extended in the same way as the bodice of the jacket.

The front and back skirts can be joined together at their outer points to make an effective dress uniform.

DECORATION

Pay attention to epaulettes, decorative braiding, sashes, buttons and belts to give your uniform jacket the correct flavour of the period and the particular army you are trying to portray.

Field soldiers' uniforms need little adornment; accessories complete the outfit.

SIMPLE WAISTCOAT

WAISTCOAT LENGTHS VARY AT THE FRONT ACCORDING TO THEIR PERIOD; THE BACKS, HOWEVER, REMAIN THE SAME, FINISHING APPROXIMATELY 6CM ($2\frac{1}{2}$IN) BELOW THE WAIST.

MEASUREMENTS

- follow instructions given for bodice on p49 • multiply length by 2 to establish amount of fabric required
- allow 6–8cm (2½–3in) extra fabric for finishing the front neck, centre edges and hems

CUTTING INSTRUCTIONS

- make a paper or cloth block pattern from the bodice measurements • cut one back and two front pieces in outer and lining fabric • allow for an overlap on front pieces for buttons and buttonholes • cut facings in outer fabric for centre front edges

ONE

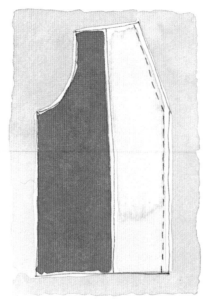

Stiffen the front facings with canvas or vilene. Place facings on centre edge of front pieces, right sides together, and machine. Open out flat and sew a hem by hand all along both pieces.

TWO

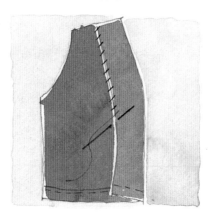

Turn facings over to wrong side of front pieces and iron the seam edges flat. Slipstitch the open edge in place.

THREE

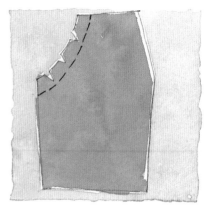

With right sides together, machine the lining to the front pieces at the armholes. Trim the lining to shape, leaving a 1cm (⅜in) seam allowance all round. Notch the armhole seam, turn the lining over to the inside and press the armhole seams flat.

FOUR

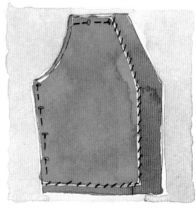

Pin the lining in place all round. Turn in the lining about 1.5cm (⅝in) at the neck and hem, and about 4cm (1½in) at the front edges.

Hand sew it in place. Tack the shoulder and side seams together to keep the lining from moving.

SEVEN

EIGHT

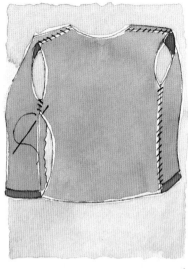

FIVE

Machine the lining to the back piece at the neck, armholes and hem. Cut the seam allowances down to 1cm (⅜in) and notch the seams to allow the curves to lie flat.

SIX

Turn the material through the side openings to the right side. Press the neck, armholes and hem flat and pin the lining to the back.

Put the right sides of the back and fronts together and position ties at the side seams at waist level if required. Join the shoulder seams and side seams, only taking in the outer fabric of the back piece. Press the seams back, not open.

Bring the back lining over and turn it to encase the seams. Sew the lining by hand onto the machining.

BASIC SHAPES △ UNDERWEAR

WHEN CONSTRUCTING PERIOD COSTUMES WE NEED TO LOOK AT WHAT WENT UNDERNEATH. MANY GARMENTS WERE SHAPED WITH THICK PADDING AND WHALEBONES, WHICH COULD BE A NIGHTMARE TO MAKE, BUT HERE ARE SOME SHORT CUTS.

Special undergarments are often required to provide the necessary shaping for period costumes but they can also be stage costumes in themselves, as in Olwen Wymark's stage adaptation of Emile Zola's novel Nana.

FRILLED PETTICOAT

THE PETTICOAT IS MADE IN THE SAME WAY AS A RECTANGLE SKIRT (SEE PAGE 22). THE SIMPLE ADDITION OF A WIDE FRILL ON THE BOTTOM OF THE PETTICOAT WILL OFTEN BE ENOUGH TO MAKE THE SKIRT STAND OUT.

MEASUREMENTS

• follow instructions given for rectangle skirt on p22 • decide on depth of frill • multiply the circumference of the petticoat's hem by 3 to establish length of frill

CUTTING INSTRUCTIONS

• follow instructions given for rectangle skirt on p22 • cut as many strips of frill as you need to make up the required length

ONE

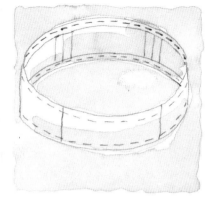

Sew the frill pieces of material together to make one continuous circle, making sure all the seams are on the wrong side. Finish both edges of the frill with a small hem.

TWO

Divide the skirt and frill into four, and mark. Run a gathering thread through the frill 1cm (½in) in from one edge, starting and finishing at the quarter marks.

THREE

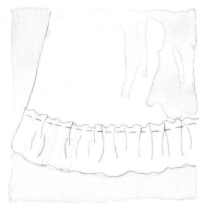

Place the hem edge of the frill against the hem edge of the petticoat and pin the frill in place, matching the quarter marks you made. Draw up the gathering threads evenly and pin the frill in place. Machine it to the petticoat by stitching through the gathering.

BONED PETTICOAT

FOR SKIRTS LIKE CRINOLINES YOU NEED A BONED PETTICOAT. THIS HAS CHANNELS SEWN ROUND IT TO ALLOW BONES TO BE SLOTTED THROUGH. IT IS IMPORTANT THAT THE HEIGHT OF EACH CHANNEL IS CONSISTENT ALL ROUND THE PETTICOAT. YOU WILL PROBABLY BE ABLE TO GET AWAY WITH USING JUST TWO CHANNELS.

MEASUREMENTS
- follow instructions given for rectangle skirt on p22
- multiply circumference of the petticoat's hem by 2 to establish quantity of bones and channelling tape required

CUTTING INSTRUCTIONS
- follow instructions given for rectangle skirt on p22

ONE

Make the first channel at the bottom of the petticoat by sewing a hem the width of the bone. Leave an opening to feed the bone in place.

TWO

Measure up from the hem to find the position of the second channel, and mark it all round the petticoat. Use a cotton tape to make the channel.

THREE

Place the tape at the level of your mark, and machine both edges, leaving an opening to slot the bone through.

FOUR

Slot the plastic bones through the channels, joining them together with plastic electrical tape or surgical tape, with one piece overlapping the other.

CORSET

MAKING CORSETS IS AN ART IN ITSELF AND NOT WITHIN THE SCOPE OF THIS BOOK. BONING THE GARMENT OR BODICE YOU ARE MAKING IS A MUCH EASIER OPTION.

MEASUREMENTS

• follow instructions given for bodice on p49 • for bones for side seams of a bodice, measure from waist up to 1cm (½in) below armhole edge • for bones for centre back and front seams, measure from top to bottom

CUTTING INSTRUCTIONS

• follow instructions given for bodice on p49 • cut the bones to the length required

ONE

Machine together two pieces of 1cm (½in) tape, one on top of the other, along both edges, to make a length of channelling to slot the bones into. It is useful to keep a quantity of this made up in your sewing box.

TWO

Cut the bones to the length required. Cover their ends with sticky tape and insert them into the channelled tape. Cut the tape, leaving enough to turn over and encase the ends of the bone.

THREE

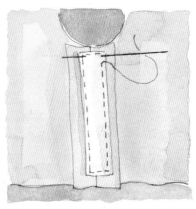

Pin the encased bones into position on the inside of the seams you wish to bone. Sew along either side of the tape to anchor it to the garment, making sure you sew firmly across the top and bottom to stop the bones coming out.

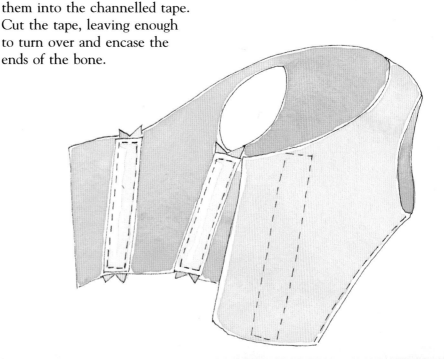

HIP ROLL

Hip rolls are long, padded sausage-shaped rolls which rest on the hips and are tied at the front with tapes. A gap is left at the front of the body to allow the skirt to hang flat.

MEASUREMENTS

• waist • hips

CUTTING INSTRUCTIONS

• cut a rectangle of soft fabric 30cm (12in) wide and length required to fit round the wearer • allow 1cm (½in) for turnings and seams

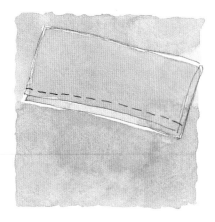

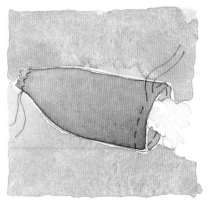

Fold the material over to make a tube 15cm (6in) wide and machine a seam 1cm (½in) in from the raw edge. Turn the tube so that the seam is on the inside. Neaten the open ends.

Run a gathering thread round the openings at both ends. Draw up the gathers at one end and sew firmly into place to close the circle. Stuff the roll firmly with wadding, pushing it in through the open end. For economy, you can use old cut-up tights. Draw up the gathering threads tightly at the open end and sew firmly to close the roll. Sew tapes onto the ends for ties.

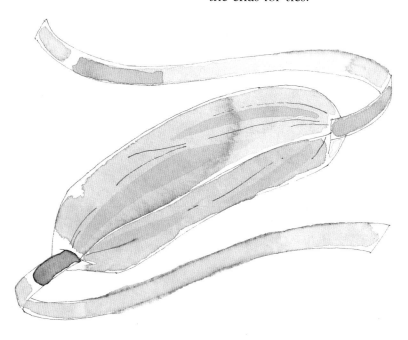

HIP PAD

HIP PADS ARE MADE IN THE SHAPE OF A LARGE U, MOST OF THE PADDING BEING AT THE TOP OF THE U, WHICH IS THE SIDE WORN AT THE WAIST. MAKE THEM SEPARATELY IN PAIRS TO ENABLE YOU TO USE THEM ON TOP OF ONE ANOTHER TO CREATE A BUSTLE.

MEASUREMENTS
• waist • hips

CUTTING INSTRUCTIONS
• cut a U shape to size required by drawing a square or rectangle and then curving two of the corners at one end
• cut a square or rectangle, large enough to cover U shape and encase wadding

ONE
Use soft cotton material to make hip pads. The size depends on how exaggerated a shape you want to achieve.

TWO

Build the pad by using wadding in layers. First put a layer of wadding all over the U shape. Start the next layer at the top, and finish it three-quarters of the way down. Start the next layer at the top and finish it half-way down. The last layer should finish a quarter of the way down. Anchor all the layers together by hand-stitching them to your material.

THREE
Lay the large square or rectangle over the padding to encase it. Pin it to fit, but don't flatten the padding.

FOUR

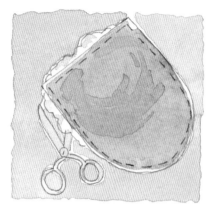

Sew the materials together 1cm (½in) in from the edge. Trim the wadding and material all round and neaten the edges to stop it fraying. Sew a tape across the top straight edge, leaving ties at either end long enough to tie round the waist.

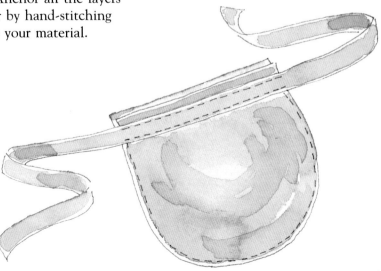

PERIOD COSTUMES

CLASSICAL

GREEK COSTUMES ARE USED FOR
PLAYS SUCH AS *OEDIPUS REX*, AS
WELL AS FOR MYTHOLOGICAL
TALES LIKE THAT OF *JASON AND
THE ARGONAUTS*. THE ROMAN
STYLE OF DRESS IS USED IN
PRODUCTIONS OF *ANTONY
AND CLEOPATRA*, AND FOR
CHARACTERS SUCH AS
PONTIUS PILATE.

This chiton has been sewn into folds and elasticated at the waist to give better control and ease of movement on stage. Braid is used to decorate the neck and hem.

Materials used by the early Greeks would probably have been linen and wool. Few accurate records of colour exist, though we know that it was used on costume borders and embroidery. We tend to assume that the main part of the costumes were white or off white. Roman clothes were made from linen, silk and wool, leather being used for belts and military uniforms. Colours were also predominantly white or off white, but often with woven borders of dark red or purple. Gold and silver threads were used in embroidery. Black and grey were worn for mourning.

GREEK

Both men and women wore chitons, the women's girded under the bust, and rectangle-style cloaks, which also served as the main head covering. Heads were often left uncovered, or a simple bandeau-style ribbon was tied round. Men wore their hair short and tightly curled around the face. Women wore their hair long and curled, often tied at the back of the neck and allowed to hang down the back or over a shoulder. Both men and women wore flat sandals of fine leather.

ROMAN

A man's garment was a tunic belted round the waist, with a purse attached to the belt. A toga was worn over the tunic by senators, and for ceremonial dress. The toga was tucked into the belt, which anchored it round the body. Women wore a chiton girded round the waist or a long tunic. Rectangular cloaks were used to cover the head in bad weather.

Men's hair was cut short and crimped. Women's hair had curls piled on top of the head and hanging down the back. Emperors, or those victorious in combat, wore circlets of laurel leaves. Both men and women wore rings and bracelets; women also wore necklaces and dangling earrings. Women wore sandals; men either wore sandals or calf-length boots of fine leather.

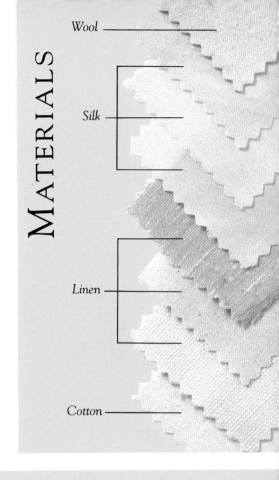

MATERIALS

Wool

Silk

Linen

Cotton

ACCESSORIES

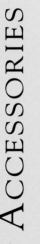

Costume tiaras are widely available or can be fashioned from wire, beads and netting.

Open sandals or boots can be worn by both men and women.

Laurel wreaths are easily made from lengths of wire. Use the leaves from artificial flowers which can be left green or sprayed a different colour.

GREEK

MAN'S COSTUME

You will need a basic chiton which can be any length from knee to ankle. A simple rectangle cloak is optional but should be 90cm (36in) wide and at least 180cm (72in) long.

This chiton has been tied by wrapping a length of leather round the arms, crossing it at the back and then belting it round the waist.

There are many Greek key patterns available as braiding to decorate the edges of the chiton. You can also decorate one edge of the cloak with the same braid.

Modern, leather, open sandals can be used.

A cloak can be worn in various ways. A popular style is to anchor one end at the shoulder and allow it to hang down the front, then pass it under one arm and back up to the shoulder you started from, anchoring it there or allowing it to fall forward.

A spear can be made from a broom handle with a cardboard cutout sprayed silver for the blade.

WOMAN'S COSTUME

T HE BASIC CHITON WAS ALSO WORN BY GREEK WOMEN, BUT WAS ANKLE LENGTH. A SIMPLE RECTANGULAR CLOAK CAN ALSO BE WORN.

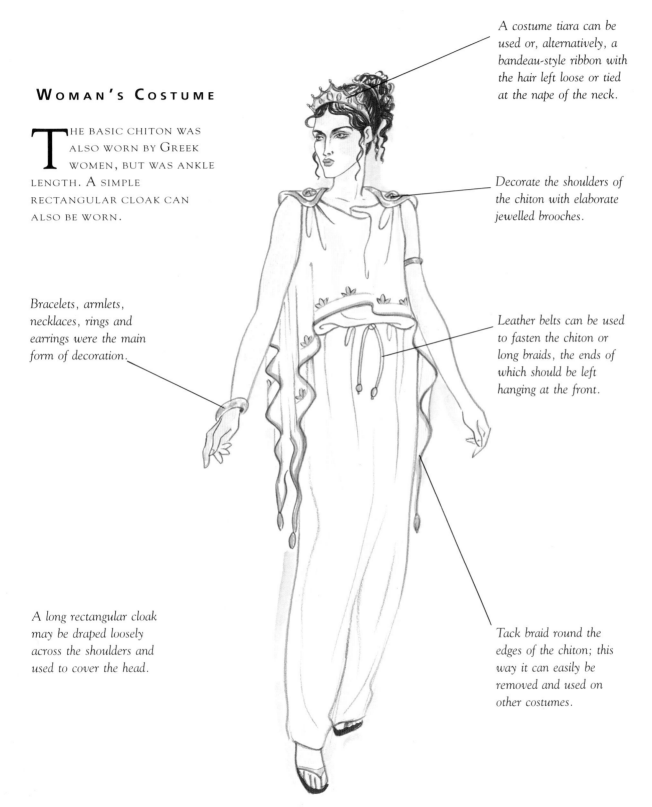

A costume tiara can be used or, alternatively, a bandeau-style ribbon with the hair left loose or tied at the nape of the neck.

Decorate the shoulders of the chiton with elaborate jewelled brooches.

Bracelets, armlets, necklaces, rings and earrings were the main form of decoration.

Leather belts can be used to fasten the chiton or long braids, the ends of which should be left hanging at the front.

A long rectangular cloak may be draped loosely across the shoulders and used to cover the head.

Tack braid round the edges of the chiton; this way it can easily be removed and used on other costumes.

ROMAN

MAN'S COSTUME

USE EITHER A BASIC
CHITON OR A T SHAPE
TUNIC WITH A SLIT
DOWN THE FRONT FOR THE
NECK. A TOGA IS SIMPLY A
RECTANGLE OF MATERIAL
APPROXIMATELY 7M (8YD)
IN LENGTH.

The neck edges, front
opening and the bottoms
of the sleeves may be
decorated with straight
braid or ribbon.

Wrap the toga
around the
wearer and have
at least one
folded pleat at
the front, then
drape it over the
left shoulder and
let it hang down
the back to calf
length.

The tunic would be belted
with a leather belt which
can also be used to keep a
toga in place.

The tunic length will be
decided by the character:
a young man or a peasant
would wear a knee-length
tunic; an older man or a
senator would wear a
full-length one.

One edge of the toga can
be decorated with the
same braid or ribbon used
on the tunic.

Boots can be left
unadorned or you can add
a dagged canvas strip to
the top edge.

WOMAN'S COSTUME

A BASIC CHITON GIRDLED AT THE WAIST IN ITS NATURAL PLACE OR UNDER THE BUST SHOULD BE WORN. ALTERNATIVELY, MAKE THE SAME TUNIC STYLE AS FOR THE MAN'S COSTUME BUT FLOOR LENGTH.

Ribbons and bandeaux were worn in the hair, which should be highly stylized in tight curls.

You can adapt the basic chiton by sewing a series of contact points along the arms. The chiton should reach from elbow to elbow or wrist to wrist and the overdrape can be omitted if preferred.

Simple rectangle-style cloaks like those of the Greeks were worn.

Tack braiding along the edge of the cloak in the same way as for the Greek costumes.

Jewellery is the main decoration – bracelets, necklaces and earrings.

Flip flops can be used or open sandals.

MEDIEVAL

THE MEDIEVAL STYLE OF DRESS IS USED IN PRODUCTIONS SUCH AS ROMEO AND JULIET, HAMLET AND BECKET. HISTORIANS DEFINE THE MIDDLE AGES AS BETWEEN THE FIFTH AND FOURTEENTH CENTURIES. HERE, IT HAS BEEN SPLIT INTO TWO DISTINCT STYLES OF DRESS: EARLY AND LATE MEDIEVAL.

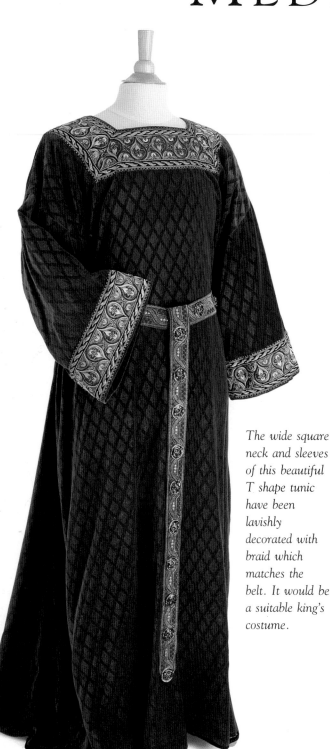

The wide square neck and sleeves of this beautiful T shape tunic have been lavishly decorated with braid which matches the belt. It would be a suitable king's costume.

Clothes were made of wool, linen, leather and fur, with decoration often woven into the fabric or embroidered on. The nobility wore bright colours – red, green, yellow and blue; ordinary people wore reddish-brown or grey. Towards the end of the medieval period, people travelled more widely and a greater variety of fabrics and colours became available. Merchants brought velvet, brocade, taffeta and silk from the East, and bold colours of scarlet, purple and bright tan became popular.

EARLY MEDIEVAL

Men wore tunics similar to those of the Romans. Nobles wore an undertunic with straight sleeves and a more flamboyant overtunic with wider sleeves. The round neckline had a slit opening at the front. A leather belt supported the wearer's purse, and leggings or baggy trousers were tied with thongs round the lower legs.

Both men and women wore a rectangular cloak, attached to their top garments by a brooch. Many men wore a short, hooded cape, similar to a monk's cowl and, for travelling, they wore a hood or a low-crowned skull cap with a turned-up brim. Their hair either hung straight down to the collar or was cut in a "pudding bowl" shape, short at the back and fringed at the front. Shoes were close fitting and made of soft leather with long, pointed toes.

Women's dresses fitted closely, with the skirt flaring out from the hips downwards. A girdle was worn round the hips. Sleeves were long and close

The hanging sleeves have been faced with a contrasting fabric and turned back to form a cuff, a feature of early medieval style. Note the lavish trimming and sumptuous fabric.

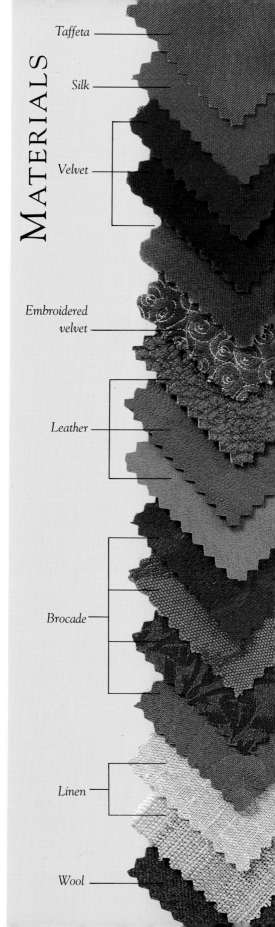

MATERIALS

Taffeta

Silk

Velvet

Embroidered velvet

Leather

Brocade

Linen

Wool

The bodice of this late medieval dress is decorated with beads and fine braids which are then laced below the bust. The sleeves are slashed open to reveal soft undersleeves.

fitting, or widened out at the wrists into a long hanging shape which reached down to the ground. Often an overdress was worn, joined to the main garment at the shoulders. It was similar to a pinafore dress, but with the sides of the bodice cut out.

Women's long hair was often plaited, and mostly hidden under a veil or headdress. Headwear varied, but often consisted of a wimple worn under a long veil, which was kept in place by a circlet of braid or metal.

LATE MEDIEVAL

Men wore padded, hip-length jackets. The padded sleeves were full at the top and tapered to the wrist. Sometimes a loose, dagged sleeve revealed the undergarment sleeve. Short shoulder cloaks were popular, the hood often being shaped into a long, pointed tail called a liripipe. Older men wore knee-length coats.

Hats had low, round crowns and padded, roll-like brims. Often folds of fabric or a liripipe hung from the hat. Hose would often have legs of different colours. Points on the shoes became more exaggerated.

Women wore dresses with high-waisted, close-fitting bodices and wide, V-shaped necklines, often trimmed with fur. Long, flowing skirts fell into a train at the back. Skirts were often so long they fell in folds on the floor, and had to be picked up and held in the hand by the wearer when walking. The tight-fitting sleeves came right down over the backs of the hands.

Women's headdresses varied from padded heart shapes to tall, cylindrical hats with elaborately wired gauze veils which stood out like butterfly's wings. Their hair was kept hidden under the headdress and veil.

ACCESSORIES

Cylinders of gold wire and fabric attached to a circlet of braid make an effective early medieval headdress. The cylinders lie on either side of the head.

Celtic-style pewter brooches have a medieval image.

A padded roll with a long cone of fabric in the centre which forms a liripipe is quite easy to make. Use a beret as a foundation.

A jewelled clasp can be used to fasten cloaks.

Attach loops to the back of suede or leather purses so that they can be threaded onto a belt.

Pointy toed shoes can be made from shaped pieces of felt glued to a bought pair of inner soles.

Use wire to create a large winged frame over which a veil can be draped and attach this to a simple cap. It should be worn towards the back of the head.

MAN'S COSTUME

USE THE T SHAPE FOR THE UNDERGARMENT OR PEASANT CLOTHES. A TOP GARMENT CAN BE MADE USING THE SAME SHAPE, OR YOU CAN USE TWO RECTANGLES OF MATERIAL TO MAKE A SIMPLE TABARD. A RECTANGLE CLOAK IS OPTIONAL.

A plain woollen cap can be worn.

The cloak requires no sewing other than neatening the edges. Use a Celtic-style clasp or brooch to fasten it at the neck.

The tabard can be either knee or full length. It only needs to be joined at the shoulder seams and the other edges neatened with small hems. Belt it at the waist.

For peasants use baggy trousers which should be criss-crossed with long shoelaces round the lower legs as thongs. Use tights or leggings for noblemen.

The neckline can be a high, round shape or that of the tunic with a slit at the centre front.

Woman's Costume

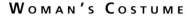

Flare out the long fitted bodice at hip level to form a skirt. The sleeves are panel shaped and extended by adding a rectangle as for the kimono. An overdress is optional and is made in the same way as the dress but without sleeves.

Decorate the neck and sleeve edges with flat braid. Make a girdle from a long piece of the same braid, or from a cord.

An overdress should be the same shape as the dress but with cutouts at the sides. To do this, draw a curve from the shoulder to the point of the bust and then out to the hip line. You can decorate the edges with braid.

The bodice should be tight fitting but without darts. To do this, cut it a little too small and lace it at the back or cut the material on the cross to help mould it to the body.

To make a feature of the bottoms of the sleeves extend them at the lower edges with rectangular shapes reaching to the floor.

MAN'S COSTUME

YOU WILL NEED A LONG PADDED DOUBLET WITH PANEL-SHAPED SLEEVES. A SHORT, HOODED CAPE IS MADE FROM A SEMI-CIRCLE FOR THE SHOULDERS AND TWO RECTANGLES FOR THE HOOD.

The rectangular hood can be extended at one corner to form a liripipe and the edges of the cloak should be dagged or scalloped.

A leather purse can be attached to a belt round the waist.

The doublet should finish at thigh level.

The sleeves can be accentuated by sewing long rectangles of material into the armholes. These should be left hanging open and decorated with dagged or scalloped edges.

Tights are worn and can have different coloured legs. Cut up coloured tights at their crotch seams and sew contrasting coloured legs together.

Shoes had exaggerated points. Use felt to create the right shape and attach it to bought insoles.

WOMAN'S COSTUME

Alter the pattern of the short fitted bodice to finish under the bust and make a wide, low, V-shaped neckline. You need a skirt with a train. The sleeves can be made from either a panel or a rectangle.

This is a difficult hat to make but you can use a padded hip roll over a beret of gold criss-cross braid. Fine voile or chiffon should be draped over the roll and under the chin.

A wide piece of braid or ribbon can be used as a decorative covering for the waist seam.

Trim the neckline and hem of the dress with fake fur or decorative edging.

Finish rectangular sleeves with small cuffs. Panel sleeves should be tight fitting and finish over the knuckles.

An under chemise and long petticoat can be worn in a contrasting colour to the dress.

16TH CENTURY

THIS LATE RENAISSANCE PERIOD
WAS A TIME OF GREAT ARTISTS
AND PLAYWRIGHTS. PLAYS USING
THIS STYLE OF DRESS INCLUDE
MANY OF SHAKESPEARE'S, *THE
WHITE DEVIL* AND *A MAN FOR
ALL SEASONS*. HERE WE CALL THE
EARLIER PERIOD TUDOR AND THE
LATER ELIZABETHAN.

This jacket clearly shows the winged shoulders which became a feature in the sixteenth century. The front has been slashed and a contrasting fabric inserted.

Materials varied from silk and satin to velvet and richly woven damask. Wool and linen were still worn by the lower classes, but merchants' dress copied that of the nobility who wore red, blue, green, turquoise and black; country folk and lower orders wore the reddish brown or greys of earlier centuries.

TUDOR

Men's costume was bulky and wide. A fine shirt was worn under a padded, straight-sleeved jacket, the neck of which was cut square or high. The jacket had a waistline and a skirt or basque pleated in soft folds to finish just above the knee. The front was left open to allow the cod piece to show through. Jacket sleeves were often slashed in panels held together by jewels or braid to show off the shirt or inner lining. A wide, loose coat was worn over the jacket. Knee length or full length for scholars, it often had a fur collar all the way to the hemline. The sleeves were short and full, and often also slashed.

The inner layer of the breeches was hose; the outer layer on the upper legs were short puffed trousers with a decorated cod piece attached by ties. Hats were flat in the crown like a beret, and had an underbrim, and often a feather on one side. They were worn at a rakish angle.

Women's dresses had a tight-fitting bodice with a very flat front. The waistline was either at the natural line or went down to a small point at the front. Necklines were very wide and square and often decorated with braid. The straight sleeves were similar to those of the medieval dress, and finished over the hand ending in a point or were turned back into a cuff. The skirt was padded underneath with a boned petticoat to

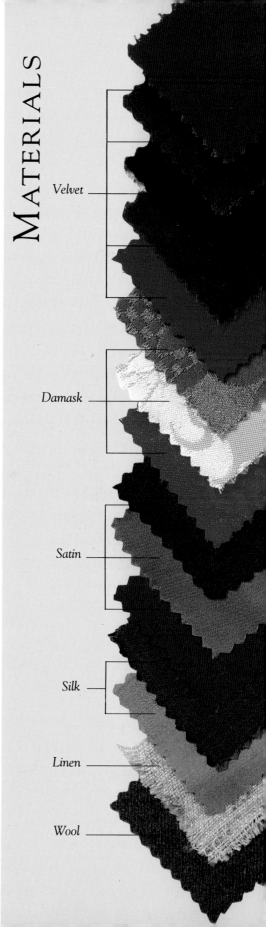

MATERIALS

Velvet

Damask

Satin

Silk

Linen

Wool

The front of this herald's tabard is appliquéed with a fleur-de-lys design. The sides and sleeve seams are left open and the garment is adorned with rope tassels.

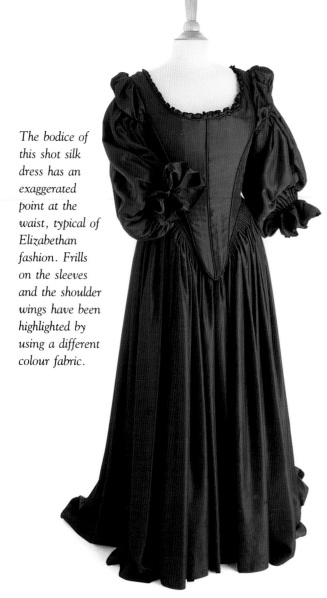

The bodice of this shot silk dress has an exaggerated point at the waist, typical of Elizabethan fashion. Frills on the sleeves and the shoulder wings have been highlighted by using a different colour fabric.

mostly hidden by the headdress. Men wore low-heeled and square-toed shoes. Women's shoes were low heeled and made of leather or velvet.

ELIZABETHAN

In the latter half of the sixteenth century men's costume became more stylized. The jacket was closer fitting, the front waist finishing in a sharp point below the natural waistline. It had a short basque attached. The shoulders extended with padded wings; sleeves were straight and slashed. Stiff, pleated ruffs adorned the high collar and the ends of the sleeves. A short circular cloak replaced the overrobe. Breeches were puffed and encased with decorative slashed panels, tights or hose still being worn on the lower legs.

For women, Queen Elizabeth I of England set the fashion for very decorative, stylized dresses. The darker colours worn earlier were gradually replaced by lighter shades of peach and cream. Padded hip rolls and boned petticoats made skirts wider at the hips. The bodice was very stiff and finished at the front waist in a very long point, often achieved by a separate front called a stomacher. Sleeves were of the melon shape, wide at the top and narrowing into the wrist, and were often padded and decorated with braid and jewels. The shoulders had padded wings. Necklines varied from a high collar to the lower square shape seen earlier in the century. Both styles were decorated with a stiff, pleated ruff. On the lower neckline it was attached at the sides and held out and up by a wire frame.

Men's hats were beret shaped or had a stiffened high crown and a small brim. Ladies still wore the band headdress with a veil attached, or a simple lace cap worn flat on the head with a point over the forehead. Men's hair became shorter, and small, pointed beards were very fashionable. Women's hair styles became higher in the front, and were often padded with false hair. The back of the hair was coiled up or worn in a bun. Ropes of pearls were worn round the neck and also draped in the hair. Both men's and women's shoes were low heeled and close fitting, made of leather or fabric to match the costume.

form a cone shape. A richly embroidered petticoat was worn on top, the top layer of the skirt being divided at the centre front to reveal it.

There were two styles of headdress. One was like a wide headband with a veil at the back. The second was very stylized and worn mainly in England. It sat on the front of the head and was known as a "Gable", because the shape resembled a gabled roof. Fabric was attached to the back and hung down over the hair.

Men's hair was worn shoulder length or short. Some men wore beards and moustaches. Women's long hair was parted in the middle and

ACCESSORIES

An Elizabethan man's hat can be made by covering stiff card with velvet.

Lace handkerchiefs were carried by both men and women.

Use netting and lace to fashion a neckpiece. Florist's wire will keep the outer edges stiff and the front opening should be fastened with velcro or press studs.

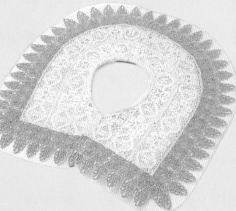

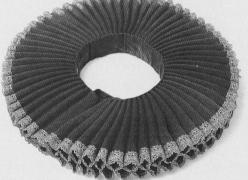

Square-toed shoes with small slashes on the front were popular in Tudor times.

Ruffs can be made in many colours and decorated with gold braiding or small pearls.

Women wore many ropes of pearls as well as brooches, rings and other jewellery.

TUDOR

MAN'S COSTUME

USE THE SHORT FITTED BODICE FOR THE JACKET AND ATTACH KNEE-LENGTH, WIDE PLEATED SKIRTS. YOU WILL ALSO NEED A FULL-SLEEVED SHIRT WITH CUFFS, A PAIR OF TIGHTS OR LEGGINGS, AND A WIDE PAIR OF SHORT, BAGGY TROUSERS. AN OVER-GARMENT CAN BE MADE FROM RECTANGLES, ALLOWING ENOUGH MATERIAL FOR IT TO FIT OVER THE JACKET.

A small ruff can be worn or allow the edge of the shirt to show.

Instead of slashing the jacket sleeves, you can sew on small ruched pieces of silk.

Cover a cricket box with fabric to make a cod piece. It can be tied in place with ribbons.

The overrobe should be knee length, the front left open to finish in curves up to the natural neckline.

Attach decorative sleeves to the overrobe. The puffed tops can have strips of ribbon or braid attached to give a slashed effect. Long rectangles can be left to hang loosely from the elbow bands.

The dress needs a wide, square neckline and can be worn with or without a collar.

WOMAN'S COSTUME

ATTACH PANEL SLEEVES TO THE SHORT FITTED BODICE. THE SKIRT CAN BE MADE EITHER IN TWO LAYERS, ONE OPENING AT THE FRONT TO REVEAL THE OTHER, OR AS ONE SKIRT USING TWO DIFFERENT FABRICS. YOU WILL ALSO NEED A PETTICOAT WITH A LOWER EDGE BONE.

Bind the neck, armholes and waist of the bodice with piping.

Stiffen the front of the bodice with vilene or canvas as well as boning the front and side seams.

A rectangular collar can be attached to an underbodice which should have a high, round neckline fastening at the front. Stiffen the edges of the collar with florist's wire and decorate with lace edging.

Sleeves should be tight and finish in a point over the knuckles.

MAN'S COSTUME

ATTACH A SHORT PANEL BASQUE TO THE SHORT FITTED BODICE FOR THE JACKET. USE RUFFS AT THE NECK AND CUFFS. YOU WILL NEED A FULL-SLEEVED SHIRT WITH CUFFS, A PAIR OF TIGHTS OR LEGGINGS, A PAIR OF SHORT, SLASHED TROUSERS AND SOME KNEE-LENGTH TAPERED ONES AS WELL.

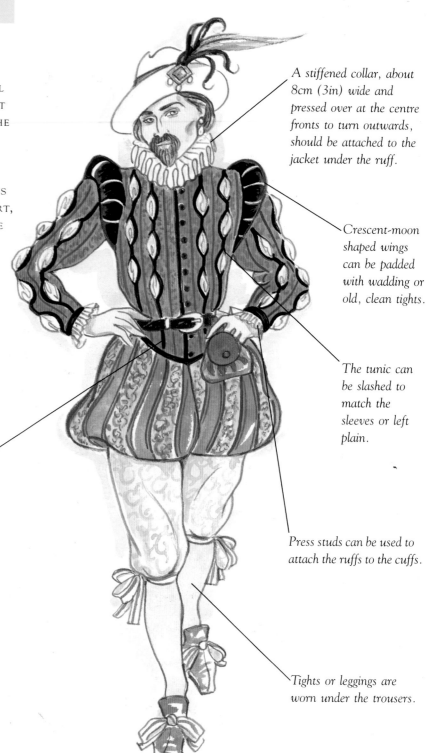

The centre front of the jacket should extend 8cm (3in) down from the natural waistline and the fronts should be stiffened with vilene or canvas.

On many jackets the basque is as short as 5cm (2in); on others it is longer and finishes at the top of the hips. It should flare out at the sides so that it fits over the short, puffed breeches.

A hip-length semi-circular cloak was commonly worn.

A stiffened collar, about 8cm (3in) wide and pressed over at the centre fronts to turn outwards, should be attached to the jacket under the ruff.

Crescent-moon shaped wings can be padded with wadding or old, clean tights.

The tunic can be slashed to match the sleeves or left plain.

Press studs can be used to attach the ruffs to the cuffs.

Tights or leggings are worn under the trousers.

WOMAN'S COSTUME

USE THE SHORT FITTED BODICE, CUTTING IT WITH CENTRE FRONT AND CENTRE BACK SEAMS AND A WIDE, SQUARE NECKLINE. YOU WILL NEED A PETTICOAT WITH A LOWER EDGE BONE AND A HIP ROLL. THE SKIRT CAN BE MADE IN ONE OR TWO LAYERS, AND YOU WILL NEED A RUFF OR LACE COLLAR FOR THE NECK.

A large ruff is needed for the neck. Instead of circular, you could attach a long strip of ruff along the back of the neck and down both front edges of the bodice neckline. Use florist's wire to make it stand up at the back.

The centre front of the bodice should extend 13cm (5in) from the natural waistline in an exaggerated point and be stiffened and boned. Sew mock slashing down the centre or simply decorate with ribbons.

Use a wire framework decorated with beads for the headdress.

The melon sleeve is a panel with the side seam edges curved outwards rather than straight. If slashed, you will need to make a double sleeve.

17TH CENTURY

THERE ARE THREE SEVENTEENTH-CENTURY STYLES THE AMATEUR GROUP MAY NEED: CAVALIER (AS WORN, FOR EXAMPLE, IN THE FILM *THE THREE MUSKETEERS*); PURITAN (AS WORN BY THE PILGRIM FATHERS); AND RESTORATION (AS WORN IN PLAYS SUCH AS *LOVE FOR LOVE*).

The cuffs and wide detachable collar of this Cavalier jacket are edged with scalloped lace. The undershirt is exposed by slashes on the front of the sleeves.

Poor people and country folk would have worn coarse woollen clothing in mainly browns and blacks. Noblemen's clothes, on the other hand, were rich and sumptuous. Early in the century they were made of satin, silk or linen, in varied colours: black and white, blue, yellow and red. Large collars and cuffs made of linen and lace decorated both men's and women's costume. By the end of the century materials included silk, satin, wool and richly embroidered brocades in colours varying from sombre browns and greys to vibrant blues, yellows and pale rose reds. In contrast, the Puritans wore clothing made of plain wool and linen in subdued tones of black, brown and grey.

CAVALIER

Men's hats had large brims and small crowns, and were decorated with ostrich feathers. Women wore lace or linen caps or hats like the men's. Men's shoes had large rosettes on the front of them. Their boots were made of fine leather and

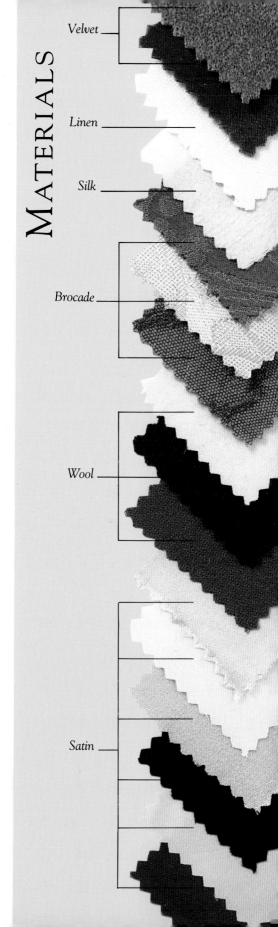

Velvet

Linen

Silk

Brocade

Wool

Satin

A combination of velvet and brocade was used to create this Cavalier style dress. The slashed sleeve effect was created by sewing strips of fabric to an undersleeve. Braid added at the elbow gives the sleeve its puffed appearance.

had a turned-down cuff. Women wore closed shoes with small heels.

Men's hair was shoulder length and often curled; they wore small pointed beards and moustaches. Women's hair was drawn back flat on the crown and divided into three. The hair on each side of the head was bunched and curled into ringlets; the back part was taken up into a high bun.

Men wore short circular cloaks with turned-back collars which were tied diagonally across the back and fastened at the front. Women wore long cloaks outdoors and long, tight-fitting gloves. They also used fans and muffs. Men wore gauntlets and used lace-edged handkerchiefs.

PURITAN

This is the style of costume associated with Oliver Cromwell's followers in Britain and with the early American settlers, the Pilgrim Fathers, who believed in a simple form of worship and style of living. Large white linen collars and cuffs were the only form of decoration.

Tall, deep-crowned hats with wide brims were worn by both men and women. Women also wore linen caps. Men wore their hair hanging naturally straight to the shoulders or cut short. Some wore beards. Women's long hair was drawn back and hidden under linen caps.

Men wore wide leather belts and their costumes had large collars which were either square, meeting together at the centre front, or wide. The wide cuffs were made of linen. Both men and women wore stockings and square-toed, low-heeled shoes. Both wore cloaks outdoors.

RESTORATION

This period of European history, named after the restoration of Charles II in 1660, was a time of great flamboyance in dress. The courts of Charles and Louis XIV of France, known as the Sun King, set the extravagant style worn by the nobility. It was echoed by the lower classes, but with less decoration on the costumes.

Men wore a tailored, flared, knee-length coat, a long waistcoat and knee breeches. Women wore a tightly fitted, stiffened bodice with a wide, round, low neckline. The skirt was full and divided at the front to show off an elaborate underskirt. Cravats took the place of collars on men's shirts. Women and peasants wore cloaks.

Men's hats were low crowned, with a large brim turned up at the back. Women wore a hat similar to the men's for riding, otherwise their heads were uncovered, though some women wore the caps favoured earlier. Men's hair was long and curled; the fashion for wearing long, curled wigs hanging down over the front and back of the shoulders became very popular. Women's hair was

This Restoration coat shows the elaborate nature of the male costume. The shape of the coat's skirt is typical of the period.

curled in ringlets, draped up at the back and sides of the head.

Men's shoes were square toed with a noticeable heel, and often decorated with large buckles or bows. Women's shoes were more delicate, higher heeled, and often made of the same fabric as the dress. The Louis heel still crops up in modern shoes. Both men and women wore stockings.

ACCESSORIES

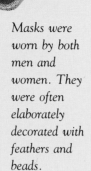

Masks were worn by both men and women. They were often elaborately decorated with feathers and beads.

Decorate a felt stetson with plumes of brightly coloured ostrich feathers.

You can imitate the turnover by attaching a wide strip of vinyl or suedette to the top of an ordinary boot.

Stocks are made by sewing layers of lace or fabric of varying lengths to a neckband.

Swords with fancy handles can be bought from toy shops.

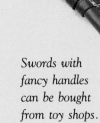

Attach rosettes and buckles to a circle of narrow elastic to fit over shoes.

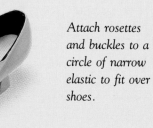

CAVALIER

MAN'S COSTUME

YOU WILL NEED A DOUBLET, BREECHES AND A FULL-SLEEVED SHIRT. THE DOUBLET CAN BE JOINED AT THE WAIST TO A BASQUE SLASHED LIKE A PEPLUM, OR CUT AS ONE TAILORED GARMENT FITTING INTO THE WAIST AND FLARING OUT OVER THE HIPS.

The large, yoke shaped collar and detachable cuffs should be edged with lace.

Extend the shoulders of the bodice beyond the normal armholes to produce wide shoulders.

Adapt ordinary gloves by attaching an extension at the wrist to make gauntlets.

Loops of braid or ribbon can be used to decorate the sleeves.

Two styles of breeches were worn: one full and drawn into a band below the knee, the other fitting more tightly and hanging straight to below the knee. Decorate the hems with loops of ribbon or braid.

A large rectangle of suedette or furnishing vinyl will transform a standard boot.

WOMAN'S COSTUME

USE THE SHORT FITTED BODICE, FINISHING ABOUT 5CM (2IN) ABOVE THE NORMAL WAISTLINE. IN SOME STYLES THE FRONT WOULD HAVE BEEN FINISHED IN A POINT; OTHERS WOULD HAVE HAD A PEPLUM BASQUE HANGING DOWN OVER THE SKIRT, JOINED TO THE WAIST WITH A STRAIGHT SEAM BEFORE THE SKIRT WAS ATTACHED TO THE BODICE.

Use a wide-rimmed felt stetson with a large ostrich feather.

The neckline can be high, like the man's, or low, cut in a wide square. Make dectachable lace cuffs and a collar.

The bodice can have a centre front seam and front darts to help with the fit. Position the darts from the point of the bust to the under-bust measurement. The seams should be boned.

The sleeves may be wide and full, drawn into bands below the elbows and finished with lace cuffs, or long and straight, finishing at the wrist with wide lace cuffs. Use a panel to make straight sleeves and a rectangle to make full sleeves, inserting elastic into the elbow bands to keep the latter in place.

A full, rectangle skirt with a back opening should be worn.

PURITAN

MAN'S COSTUME

YOU WILL NEED A DOUBLET, KNEE BREECHES AND A FULL-SLEEVED SHIRT WITH DETACHABLE CUFFS. A WOOLLEN KNEE-LENGTH CLOAK CAN BE WORN AND IS MADE FROM EITHER A RECTANGLE OR SEMI-CIRCLE. COLOURS SHOULD BE DARK AND SOMBRE.

The fitted doublet differs from the Cavalier style in that the shoulder reverts to its normal width. The doublet finishes just below the crotch, and is fastened from top to bottom at the centre front.

Puritan men gradually began to carry muskets as they travelled farther afield.

Sleeves are straight and can be made from the panel shape. Finish them at the wrist with detachable linen cuffs.

When the Puritans started to travel through rough terrains, straight boots, possibly with a plain cuff, were worn instead of shoes.

Long woollen socks or tights should be worn on the lower legs.

Make a detachable collar and cuffs. The collar can be a continuous wide circle fastening at the back or form part of a headdress as shown.

WOMAN'S COSTUME

USE THE SHORT FITTED BODICE TO CREATE THE WOMAN'S DRESS. THE BODICE IS LEFT OPEN AT THE BACK AND THE NECKLINE FOLLOWS THE NATURAL CURVE OF THE NECK. THE WAISTLINE IS IN THE NATURAL POSITION AND CUT STRAIGHT. WIDE RECTANGLES FORM THE SKIRT AND A BASIC PETTICOAT IS WORN UNDERNEATH.

Use a panel to make straight sleeves and finish with linen cuffs. Alternatively, use a rectangle to make full sleeves. Leave them ungathered at the bottom hem and cut them with enough material to fold back into a cuff finishing just below the elbow.

Women often wore linen aprons. To make one use a rectangle of cotton fabric the length of the skirt by a width of 90cm (36in). Draw the waist edge up to 45cm (18in) with a gathering thread and attach a waistband and ties as for a semi-circle cloak.

Puritan costumes should be plain with no decoration.

RESTORATION

MAN'S COSTUME

Y OU WILL NEED A FULL-SLEEVED SHIRT FINISHED WITH A FRILL, BAGGY KNEE BREECHES, A KNEE-LENGTH WAISTCOAT AND A TAILORED COAT WITH PLEATS AT THE SIDES OF ITS SKIRT.

Face patches can be worn in this period; the more dandified the man looks, the better.

Wrap a cravat around the neck from front to back, then bring the ends round to the front again and tie in a loose knot.

Wedge-shaped flaps give the illusion of pockets.

The front edges of the coat, the slit at the back, the cuffs and the pocket flaps can be decorated with braid or strips of waistcoat material.

Sew on the buttons. It isn't necessary to make all the buttonholes as the coat is worn open to show off the waistcoat.

Large baggy knee breeches help to fluff out the coat.

The waistcoat should reach to the knee and flare out at the side when viewed from the front. Buttons should run from neck to hem, though the lower ones can be left unfastened. It should be elaborately patterned.

Make the calves more shapely with padding.

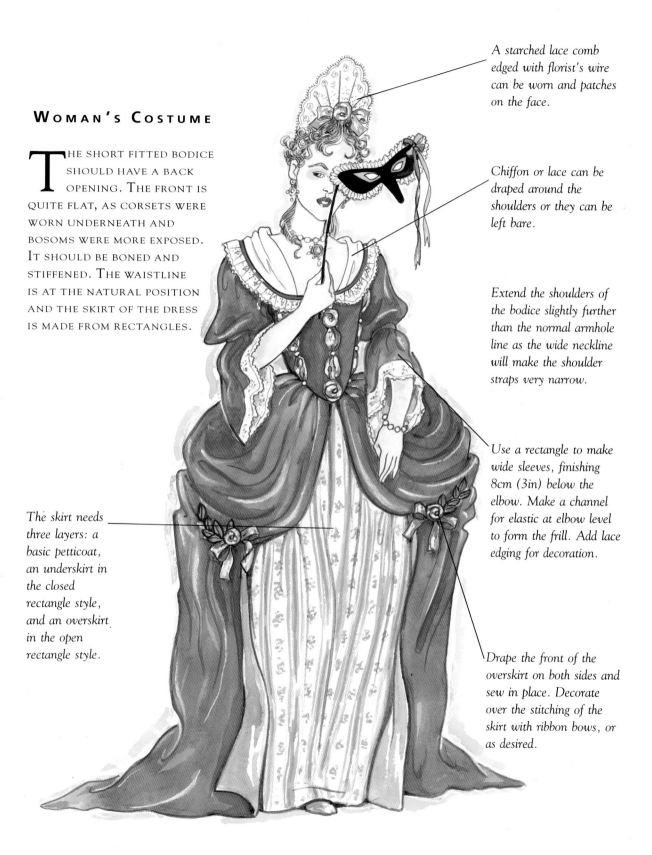

WOMAN'S COSTUME

THE SHORT FITTED BODICE SHOULD HAVE A BACK OPENING. THE FRONT IS QUITE FLAT, AS CORSETS WERE WORN UNDERNEATH AND BOSOMS WERE MORE EXPOSED. IT SHOULD BE BONED AND STIFFENED. THE WAISTLINE IS AT THE NATURAL POSITION AND THE SKIRT OF THE DRESS IS MADE FROM RECTANGLES.

A starched lace comb edged with florist's wire can be worn and patches on the face.

Chiffon or lace can be draped around the shoulders or they can be left bare.

Extend the shoulders of the bodice slightly further than the normal armhole line as the wide neckline will make the shoulder straps very narrow.

The skirt needs three layers: a basic petticoat, an underskirt in the closed rectangle style, and an overskirt in the open rectangle style.

Use a rectangle to make wide sleeves, finishing 8cm (3in) below the elbow. Make a channel for elastic at elbow level to form the frill. Add lace edging for decoration.

Drape the front of the overskirt on both sides and sew in place. Decorate over the stitching of the skirt with ribbon bows, or as desired.

18TH CENTURY

Decoration flows from the bodice seams into the skirt edges. A long shoulder train features at the back.

A VERY WIDE RANGE OF PRODUCTIONS USE THIS STYLE OF DRESS, FROM *THE MADNESS OF GEORGE III* TO *CINDERELLA*. THE STYLES OF THE EIGHTEENTH CENTURY REMAINED FAIRLY CONSTANT THROUGHOUT.

This century was a time of inventors, and the inventions in the weaving industry produced cheaper materials. The blockade of ships to America restricted the import of fine silks and lace, and American costumes were plainer than those seen in Europe. In pre-Revolutionary France, in particular, clothes were very ornate and over-decorated.

Materials included wool, silk, satin and velvet, with muslin and cotton becoming popular in the latter part of the century. Colours were varied: at the beginning of the century bright yellows, reds and greens were popular; in the later years men wore darker, more reserved colours, and striped fabrics. Women also wore striped fabrics, often with flower designs printed on, and white and printed cottons became popular.

During the first half of the century men's styles were similar to those of the seventeenth century, but after 1750 the coat became plainer, less ornate and lost its full pleats at the sides. At the front the coat curved down from the waist to finish at knee level at the back. The waistcoat extended to crotch level. Breeches fitted more tightly and finished at the knee.

Women wore a tight corset under the bodice

which was often decorated with bows and lace. Necklines were square and low, trimmed with frills of material or lace. Sleeves were fitted down to the elbow, where frills of material or lace were attached to fall over the lower arm. The skirt was very full and divided at the front to show off an elaborate underskirt. Metal panniers worn under the skirt made it stand out at the sides.

Men wore a stylized wig which was padded in rolls at the sides of the head and finished in a tied-back piece at the nape of the neck. Natural hair was worn long and tied at the nape. Women's hair was dressed high off the face and worn in curls and ringlets. In the latter half of the century highly stylized, powdered white wigs became very fashionable. Men wore tricorn hats with low crowns. Women wore frilly mop caps or wide, flat straw hats decorated with ribbon. Men wore closed leather shoes which were decorated with buckles; calf-length boots were also worn. Women's shoes had small heels and were also decorated with buckles. Women also wore a full, circular cloak with a large hood to give protection from the weather. A muff, fan and parasol completed the woman's accessories. Men carried elaborate snuffboxes and walking sticks.

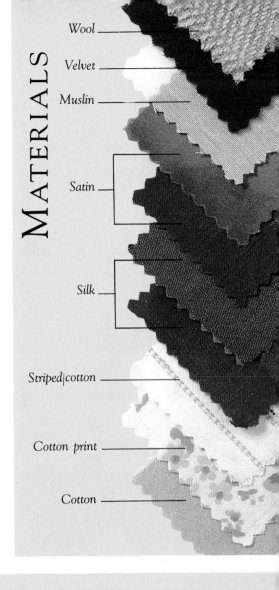

MATERIALS

Wool

Velvet

Muslin

Satin

Silk

Striped/cotton

Cotton print

Cotton

ACCESSORIES

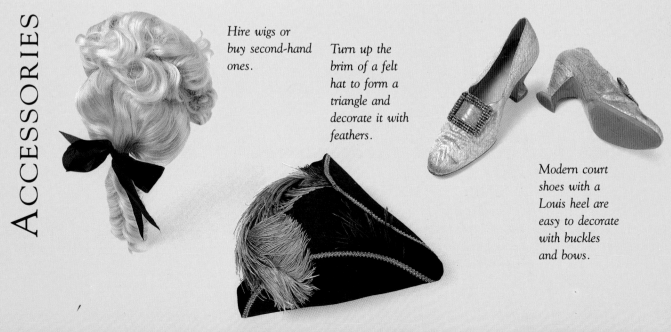

Hire wigs or buy second-hand ones.

Turn up the brim of a felt hat to form a triangle and decorate it with feathers.

Modern court shoes with a Louis heel are easy to decorate with buckles and bows.

18TH CENTURY

MAN'S COSTUME

USE THE MEASUREMENTS FOR THE LONG FITTED BODICE TO MAKE THE SWALLOW COAT. YOU WILL ALSO NEED A FULL-SLEEVED SHIRT WITH A FRILLED CUFF, A STOCK OR LACE CRAVAT, A WAISTCOAT AND A PAIR OF TIGHT KNEE BREECHES.

A stock is a rectangle of material to which frills of various lengths are attached at the front.

The coat collar is made from a rectangle and should be stiffened. It can either stand straight up or be folded over and pressed.

The cuffs of the coat should be 10cm (4in) when finished.

The waistcoat should be crotch length, and the sides flared out slightly from the waist. It is buttoned from the waist up, and needs small pocket flaps.

Decorate the front of the waistcoat with ornate braiding or use richly decorative material.

A fob watch can be worn suspended from a belt.

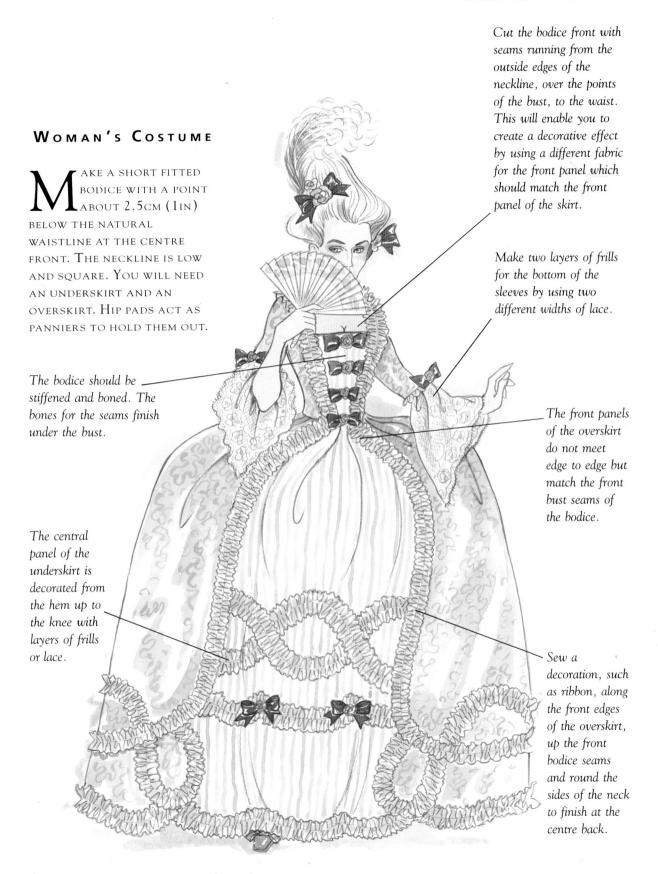

Cut the bodice front with seams running from the outside edges of the neckline, over the points of the bust, to the waist. This will enable you to create a decorative effect by using a different fabric for the front panel which should match the front panel of the skirt.

Make two layers of frills for the bottom of the sleeves by using two different widths of lace.

WOMAN'S COSTUME

MAKE A SHORT FITTED BODICE WITH A POINT ABOUT 2.5CM (1IN) BELOW THE NATURAL WAISTLINE AT THE CENTRE FRONT. THE NECKLINE IS LOW AND SQUARE. YOU WILL NEED AN UNDERSKIRT AND AN OVERSKIRT. HIP PADS ACT AS PANNIERS TO HOLD THEM OUT.

The bodice should be stiffened and boned. The bones for the seams finish under the bust.

The front panels of the overskirt do not meet edge to edge but match the front bust seams of the bodice.

The central panel of the underskirt is decorated from the hem up to the knee with layers of frills or lace.

Sew a decoration, such as ribbon, along the front edges of the overskirt, up the front bodice seams and round the sides of the neck to finish at the centre back.

19TH CENTURY

THE NINETEENTH CENTURY WAS A TIME OF GREAT CHANGE AND THE SETTING OF A WIDE RANGE OF PLAYS, INCLUDING WORKS BY CHEKHOV, PINERO AND OSCAR WILDE. THE EARLY EMPIRE (OR NAPOLEONIC) STYLE CHANGED DRAMATICALLY IN MID-CENTURY AND DEVELOPED INTO THE DISTINCTIVE FASHION OF THE VICTORIANS.

This empire dress has been made in two layers. A simple high-waisted underdress is trimmed with velvet to match the overdress. Co-ordinating braid finishes off the outfit.

Men's clothing was made from wool, velvet and cashmere, in subdued tones of grey, brown and black, the waistcoat being the only ostentatious part of the costume. Striped material was used for trousers in the latter part of the century. Women's clothing was made from cotton muslin, silk, satin, taffeta, organza and a woollen material called alpaca. Colours for women's clothes varied: white was the basis of many printed fabrics. Stripes and plaids were popular, as were pastel shades of green and lilac. Housekeepers and governesses wore black and dark mauve.

EMPIRE

At the beginning of the nineteenth century the shaped coat was cropped to a square across the front at waist level, and hung down in tails at the back – the forerunner of the evening dress tail coat we see today. The jacket had revers-style lapels and collar, the latter often made of velvet; the sleeves were made in two pieces and finished straight to the wrist, with a small cuff attached at the bottom of the sleeve. A waistcoat with revers was worn under the jacket, and round the neck of the shirt a stiff, stand-up collar had a piece of material tied at the front in a bow. Trousers were tight and ankle length.

Women's Empire dresses had short, fitted, low-necked bodices with a high waistline and softly

This frock coat has narrow silk braid sewn onto the revers, front edges and cuffs. The finishing touch is the addition of silk buttons.

MATERIALS

Tartan ribbon

Velvet

Cotton

Silk

Satin

Taffeta

gathered skirts. Sleeves were either short and puffed or long and tight fitting with short puffed tops. Corsets were not worn.

By mid-century a dramatic change had taken place, with tight-fitting bodices and corsets returning. The waistline was cut with a point at the front similar to the Elizabethan style. Necklines were wide, low and off-the-shoulder, often decorated with flounces of lace, or fitted close to the natural neckline and finished with a lace collar. The crinoline skirt was achieved by a

A distinctive style has been created on this late-19th century jacket and skirt by the cleverly placed braiding and the use of tassels. A simple blouse worn underneath complements the outfit.

hooped petticoat that held the skirt out into a wide, rounded shape. The skirt was often made in tiered layers placed one on top of another, and edged with ruched lace or fabric. Sleeves were either short and puffed, and covered by the collar flounces, or straight and fitted, with a cuff.

VICTORIAN

As the century progressed men's costume became more practical. The tailed coat had a front skirt attached to it and became what is known as a frock coat. However, shorter jackets, similar to those of today, were also worn. They were made of woollen cloth and buttoned high up the chest. Trousers hung loose from the top and tapered towards the hems. Knickerbockers – loose trousers finishing over the calf in a fitted band – were worn with long socks and boots. Shirts were made collarless and different types of stiff collar – wing, rounded and straight – were attached with collar studs. Various styles of bows and cravats were worn at the neck.

With the invention of the sewing machine in America women's costume developed in different ways, practical styles evolving as well as impractical ones. Separate skirts with bustles were worn with high-necked blouses decorated with pin tucks, and leg of mutton sleeves, full at the top of the arm and narrowing to the wrist. Tight-fitting jackets matching the skirts saw the start of women's suits. Dresses had tight-fitting bodices, with the front waistline finishing below the natural waist in a point. High cut, the bodice was finished with a small stand-up collar, and an inner lace collar protruded over the top. The bodice was fastened at the front with small buttons. Evening dresses had low, rounded necklines at the back and front, and either puffed sleeves or were sleeveless. A wired under-cage called a bustle held the skirt out at the back. The skirt was often made in two layers, the top layer being draped up at the sides to make an apron shape. The back was pleated to fall over the bustle, and the hemline was decorated with pleated frills, which matched those that decorated the bottoms of sleeves, if worn.

ACCESSORIES

Fob watches were carried in waistcoat pockets, attached by chains, often with lucky charms, to the waistcoat buttonholes.

Heavily beaded drawstring purses together with fans, muffs, parasols and umbrellas were often carried.

Bonnets were prettily trimmed with lace and ribbons. Large hairnets held the hair tidily at the back of the head.

Silver-topped black canes were favoured by gentlemen.

Button or lace-up ankle boots were popular.

Top hats typify this century.

EMPIRE

MAN'S COSTUME

YOU WILL NEED TAPERED TROUSERS, A MODERN WHITE SHIRT, A WAISTCOAT FINISHING JUST BELOW THE NATURAL WAISTLINE AND A COAT WITH TAILS AT THE BACK. AN OVERCOAT IS OPTIONAL.

Top hats became popular at this time and had slightly wider brims than modern top hats.

Adapt a modern white shirt by turning up the collar and tying it in place with a length of material which should be fastened at the front in a bow.

The empire coat is made from a short fitted bodice with two panel-shaped tails at the back. Velvet revers can be added. Use a modern pattern for the sleeves.

As an alternative to an overcoat, adapt a full-length circular cloak by adding two shorter layers, one to wrist level, the other to the upper arm. All three layers should be joined together at the neck edge.

Small cuffs can be added in the same material as the coat or in velvet. They should lie flat against the sleeve.

The trousers should be tapered or you can use stretch ski pants.

Use modern lace-up shoes.

WOMAN'S COSTUME

USE THE SHORT FITTED BODICE BUT FINISH IT AT THE UNDER-BUST MEASUREMENT LINE. THE BODICE FITS QUITE TIGHTLY, HAS A WIDE, LOW NECKLINE AND A CENTRE BACK OPENING. THE SKIRT IS MADE FROM TWO RECTANGLES.

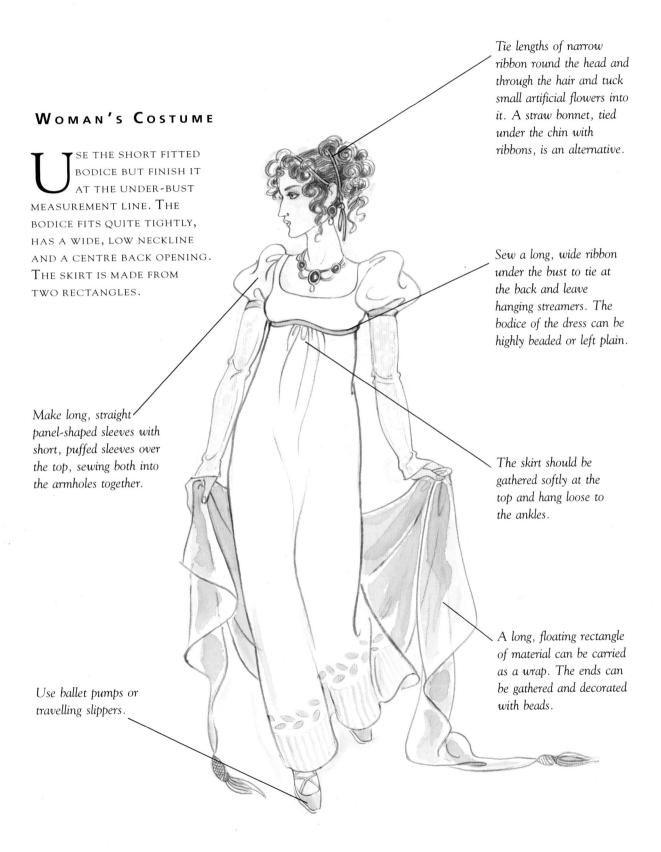

Tie lengths of narrow ribbon round the head and through the hair and tuck small artificial flowers into it. A straw bonnet, tied under the chin with ribbons, is an alternative.

Sew a long, wide ribbon under the bust to tie at the back and leave hanging streamers. The bodice of the dress can be highly beaded or left plain.

Make long, straight panel-shaped sleeves with short, puffed sleeves over the top, sewing both into the armholes together.

The skirt should be gathered softly at the top and hang loose to the ankles.

Use ballet pumps or travelling slippers.

A long, floating rectangle of material can be carried as a wrap. The ends can be gathered and decorated with beads.

MAN'S COSTUME

Tapered trousers, a waist-length coat with back tails, a waistcoat, a modern dress shirt and a bow tie are suitable for a 19th-century man's formal evening attire.

White bow ties, both large and small, were extremely popular.

Modern white dress shirts come in a variety of designs. The decorative front panel of the shirt helps to give the rather austere costume some decoration.

Grey velvet has been added to the jacket revers for decorative impact. Since men's costume at this time was rather uniform, touches such as this and the patterned shirt help to give them some distinguishing features.

A waistcoat with a low scooped neckline and no revers is worn under the jacket.

Black became the standard colour for formal evening dress for gentlemen.

WOMAN'S COSTUME

USE THE SHORT FITTED BODICE WITH THE CENTRE FRONT FINISHING 8CM (3IN) BELOW THE NATURAL WAISTLINE. IT SHOULD HAVE DARTS TO MAKE IT TIGHT FITTING, A BACK OPENING AND A WIDE, LOW NECKLINE. THE SKIRT IS MADE IN THREE LAYERS OF REDUCING LENGTH AND A BONED PETTICOAT IS WORN UNDERNEATH TO HOLD THEM OUT.

Long ringlets on either side of the face were fashionable.

Sew wide decorative lace all round the neckline; here it matched the hem decoration on each of the skirt layers.

Short puffed sleeves can be made from rectangles of fabric.

Long gloves and a fan, together with a dance card, can be used with evening wear.

Make all three layers of the skirt separately. Use gathering threads to draw up the waist of each to the correct size and tack together. Finally, attach a waistband.

VICTORIAN

MAN'S COSTUME

Y OU WILL NEED TAPERED TROUSERS, A MODERN WHITE SHIRT, A WAIST-LENGTH WAISTCOAT WITH REVERS AND POINTED FRONTS, AND A DOUBLE-BREASTED FROCK COAT.

Use a modern top hat.

The shirt collar should be turned up to make a winged collar and kept in place with a bow tie or cravat.

Use plain ribbon to edge the lapels of the coat. The back collar can be faced with velvet or fabric to match the waistcoat.

For a more casual look, adapt a modern tweed jacket by buttoning it higher at the front and wearing it with a flat cap.

Waistcoats with pointed fronts were becoming fashionable at this time.

Make tapered trousers or use stretch ski pants. The stirrups should go outside the shoes.

Walking sticks with decorative top pieces were carried.

Use modern lace-up shoes.

WOMAN'S COSTUME

USE THE SHORT FITTED BODICE WITH THE WAISTLINE 5CM (2IN) BELOW THE NATURAL LINE AT THE CENTRE FRONT. IT SHOULD HAVE DARTS AND BE BONED. THE SKIRT IS TWO LAYERS, BOTH MADE FROM THREE RECTANGLES OF MATERIAL AND MADE UP SEPARATELY. THE UNDERSKIRT SHOULD BE ANKLE LENGTH AND THE OVERSKIRT CALF LENGTH. USE HIP PADS FOR THE BUSTLE.

The bodice and the sleeves can be pin tucked if desired. The neckline can also be low and trimmed with a lace frill.

Sew channelling tape down the inside of the overskirt's side seams through which draw tapes may be slotted to raise the sides of the skirt.

Use low-heeled court shoes.

Perch a small, straw hat on top of the head, angle it forwards and decorate it with ribbon. Larger hats can also be used.

Add a stand-up collar, trimmed with pleated lace. The sleeves can be trimmed with lace too.

The sleeves can be very full, gathered at the top and narrowing towards the wrist, or narrow panel shaped.

Decorate the hem of the top skirt with pleated ribbon or braid.

An umbrella with a long handle and a spike can be decorated with pleated ribbon or lace round the top edge to create a parasol.

20TH CENTURY

PLAYS SET IN THIS CENTURY
INCLUDE THOSE OF NOEL COWARD
AND TENNESSEE WILLIAMS. IT IS
EASIEST TO ADAPT EXISTING
CLOTHES AND MOST OF THE
STYLES CAN BE PUT TOGETHER BY
ROOTING THROUGH ELDERLY
RELATIVES' WARDROBES, BY
SEEKING OUT SPECIALIST OLD
CLOTHES SHOPS, OR BY VISITING
THE LOCAL CHARITY SHOPS AND
FLEA MARKETS.

Lingerie satin was used to make this 1930s dress. The voluptuous three-quarter length jacket has dolman sleeves and the hemline is gathered in at the back and a tassel attached.

This century, with its momentous events, has had a great influence on styles of dress. In previous centuries a style of costume depicted a certain era, whereas in the latter part of this century, styles change from season to season. The American film industry set the fashion for many ordinary people. They copied the clothes and make-up of stars like Clara Bow in the 1920s and this trend has continued. Modern television and cinema give a clear picture of clothes throughout this century, in all parts of the world. Studying old movies and newsreels is a good way of researching costume.

The three-piece suit worn by men throughout this century has not changed a great deal. The waistcoat may or may not be worn with the suit, and sometimes is worn over a shirt with casual trousers. The main differences over the years are in the buttoning of the jackets and in cut of the trousers. Hairstyles and hats often date a costume. In the 1930s and 1940s the trilby hat was popular, particularly in England. The flat cap has been worn throughout the century; the bowler hat worn by Charlie Chaplin in the 1930s still distinguishes many city workers.

For women's clothing, shoes and the length of the skirt can set the syle. Stiletto heels and pointed toes denote the 1950s; platform shoes and tight-fitting knee boots the 1970s. Make-up and hairstyles are also important in creating the style you wish to achieve.

Most twentieth-century styles can still be purchased and they periodically come back into fashion. It is how you put the items of clothing together which sets the period.

MATERIALS

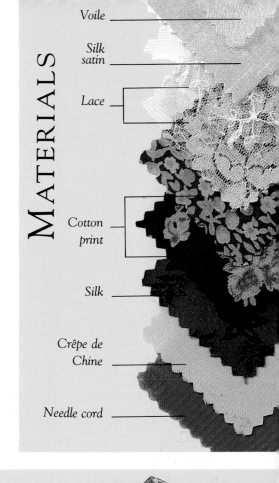

Voile

Silk satin

Lace

Cotton print

Silk

Crêpe de Chine

Needle cord

ACCESSORIES

Bowler hats were worn by smart middle-class gentlemen everywhere.

Cravats were worn in a variety of patterns.

Outrageously high platform shoes, often in patent leather, are a trademark of the 1970s.

Plastic was a new material in the 1920s and was used to make a variety of objects, such as this handbag.

AT THE BEGINNING OF THE CENTURY BUSTLES DISAPPEARED AND WOMEN'S SILHOUETTE BECAME S SHAPED, WITH A FULL BUST, WASP WAIST AND EXAGGERATED BOTTOM. THE SHAPE WAS ACHIEVED WITH CORSETS. MEN'S FASHION BECAME LESS FORMAL WITH THE FROCK COAT GOING OUT OF FAVOUR AND THE AMERICAN THREE-PIECE LOUNGE SUIT BECOMING WIDELY POPULAR.

Soft peaked flat caps were worn for casual occasions instead of a bowler hat.

The high, stiff shirt collar remained popular until World War I when soft, turned-down collars came into fashion. These were worn with ties, the whole effect being similar to that of today.

Country gentlemen wore tweed sports jackets which were an adaptation of the riding jacket. They often had large, buttoned pockets at hip level and were single breasted and fitted at the waist.

Tweed became a popular fabric and was used for both lounge suits and country and sports wear.

Knickerbockers were tucked into thick woollen knee socks. By the start of the 1920s, they were often worn with a knitted fairisle pullover and checked socks, originally for playing golf but also for other leisure activities.

Bowler hats were smart and worn by middle-class gentlemen everywhere.

Men were usually cleanshaven except for moustaches.

Motorcars were coming into use and both men and women wore protective overcoats.

Large hats were held in place with gauzy veils for motoring.

High-collared white blouses with decorated fronts were tucked loosely into A line skirts which skimmed the hips and flared at the hem, usually with a slight train at the back.

Skirts gradually became tubular and by the end of the 1910s were a couple of inches above the ankle.

1920s

CLOTHES BECAME MORE RELAXED IN THE 1920S, ALLOWING WOMEN, FOR THE FIRST TIME, TO MOVE WITH EASE. MEN'S FORMAL SUITS AND STARCHED COLLARS WERE REPLACED BY MORE CASUAL CLOTHES, AND A FASHIONABLE YOUNG MAN'S WEEKEND WARDROBE WOULD INCLUDE SPECIAL OUTFITS FOR SPORTS SUCH AS TENNIS AND GOLF.

The ensemble is completed by a straw boater worn at a jaunty angle.

A modern white shirt can be worn, open at the neck, with a silk scarf tied cravat-style.

A V-necked sweater with a coloured neckline (a modern cricket sweater would be ideal) is worn under a striped blazer.

Very wide trousers called Oxford bags came into fashion in the late 1920s. A pair of cricket flannels could be used.

This costume, without the tennis racket, would be equally suitable for boating.

The close-fitting hat fits snugly over the new, short hairstyle. This 1920s cloche is decorated with a broad ribbon tied in a large bow; a narrow silk scarf could be used instead.

The pinstriped suit, flash tie and soft hat with the brim turned down epitomize the typical gangster look of the 1920s. Modern clothes could be used to create it.

Flamboyant jewellery, such as dangling earrings and long strings of beads, contrast with the simple lines of the clothes.

The violin case was the gangster's badge of office – it carried a sawn-off shotgun!

The feather boa, worn throughout the 19th century and especially fashionable in its last decade, enjoyed a revival in the 1920s.

Shoes with a bar that buttoned or buckled over the instep were very fashionable.

Note the turn-ups on the trousers and the lack of spats – the latter were considered old-fashioned by the mid-1920s.

1930s

Men's clothes were cut to emphasize the slimness of the hips and the width of the shoulders; double-breasted suits were especially popular. Women's clothes had a softer outline than in the previous decade. For day wear this was balanced by small tilted hats and clutch bags carried under the arm.

Men still wore hats out of doors on all occasions. This is a soft, Homburg style with a bound brim.

The hair is flat and neat, and drawn severely back into a bun.

The double-breasted suit has wide lapels and long, wide trousers with turn-ups. It is worn with a waistcoat and a shirt with a button-down collar. The use of tweed material reflects the increasing informality in dress as the century progressed.

Dresses, especially evening dresses like this daring backless model, were cut on the cross to enable the fabric to drape in soft folds like the gowns depicted on classical statues.

PERIOD COSTUMES

1940s

BOTH MEN'S AND WOMEN'S CLOTHES HAD A CHARACTERISTIC SQUARE OUTLINE, WITH SHOULDER PADS. SKIRTS WERE SHORT AND PRACTICAL, AND THE MASCULINE EFFECT OF WOMEN'S CLOTHES WAS SOFTENED BY LONGER AND MORE ELABORATE HAIRSTYLES. IT WAS THE FIRST DECADE IN WHICH IT WAS COMMON PLACE FOR WOMEN TO WEAR TROUSERS.

Women's clothes were severe and functional, with a military look, echoing the man's uniform.

The hat is masculine, though its bright colour and feminine veil add a touch of glamour. Underneath it the hair would be swept up and rolled back at the front to give height. Note the shoulder bag.

The open-toed shoes have platform soles, thick high heels and ankle-straps. Wedge-heeled shoes made from lizard or crocodile skin were also popular.

Out of uniform men wore single-breasted suits with narrower trousers than in the previous decade, and no turn-ups, to save fabric.

Military uniforms were made of thick, coarse cloth, khaki (shown here) being the colour of the army. A determined hunt round old clothes' shops or relatives' attics might reveal some genuine articles.

PERIOD COSTUMES

1950s

IN 1947 WOMEN'S FASHIONS WERE REVOLUTIONIZED BY DIOR'S 'NEW LOOK', WITH NIPPED-IN WAISTS AND LONG, FULL SKIRTS, AND THIS DESIGN WAS WORN THROUGHOUT THE 1950S. AN ALTERNATIVE STYLE HAD A MID-CALF LENGTH STRAIGHT SKIRT, WITH A PLEAT OR SLIT IN THE BACK TO ALLOW FOR MOVEMENT. THIS WAS ALSO WORN WITH A FITTED BODICE AND NARROW WAIST.

Clothes were elegant and formal, with the emphasis on good grooming. Small, neat hats covered tidy hairstyles – hats and gloves were worn on almost every occasion. This woman, with her long, white gloves, could be dressed for attending a wedding or perhaps a garden party.

The long, slender umbrella with its spiked tip and open top was a fashionable accessory.

During the decade shoes became lighter, with thin soles, pointed toes and high, 'stiletto' heels.

Jewellery was neat – plain round earrings, a short strand or two of pearls – and women did not consider themselves properly dressed without it.

This dress shows both styles of 1950s' skirts. A full, gathered overskirt is held up in front to reveal a slender, 'pencil-slim' skirt beneath. The little cap sleeves were very popular.

The teddy boy, with his long drape jacket cut like a frock coat, was a product of the 1950s. He wore a fancy shirt and waistcoat with a bootlace tie, and his hairstyle was elaborately styled with grease into a quiff. Long sideburns were also worn.

His partner is dressed for dancing – this was the birth of the rock 'n' roll era. Note her fashionable pony-tail hairdo.

The cardigan is worn back to front and the sleeves pushed up to the fashionable three-quarter length.

Narrow drainpipe trousers, white socks and black suede shoes with thick crepe soles completed the outfit.

A narrow waist is emphasized by a broad belt and the skirt is very full, held out by layers of flounced petticoats.

On her feet she wears short socks and flat, 'ballerina' pumps, ideal for jiving.

YOUNG LONDON-BASED DESIGNERS LIKE MARY QUANT STARTED A FASHION REVOLUTION IN THE 1960s, CREATING YOUTHFUL, AFFORDABLE CLOTHES FOR THE FIRST TIME IN HISTORY. HEMLINES STARTED TO RISE IN 1963, TO BECOME THE SHORTEST OF MINI-SKIRTS BY 1967–8.

This modified Beatle haircut is typical of the decade. Men's clothing became more colourful and ties might be printed in bright paisley or pop art patterns.

Early 1960s' beehive hairstyles were replaced by short, straight, geometric Sassoon cuts by the middle of the decade. Eyes were heavily accentuated with make-up; lipstick was very pale.

Suits were narrow cut, with fitted single-breasted jackets and narrow lapels. Trousers did not have turn-ups.

The simple, childlike dress skims the hips and finishes at mid-thigh level. Its neat collar is trimmed by a Mary Quant logo brooch.

The Beatles started a trend for collarless jackets, and for wearing polo-necked jumpers instead of shirts and ties.

Long, patterned white tights cover the legs; the shoes have square toes and low, chunky heels. Knee-length boots were also worn with mini-skirts.

Men often wore elastic-sided ankle boots with pointed toes. These were called Chelsea boots.

PERIOD COSTUMES

1970s

Conventional ways of life were rejected by many young people in the 1970s, and this was reflected in their dress. Ideas were borrowed from other eras and other cultures, from Laura Ashley's Victorian- and Edwardian-inspired clothes to the ethnic beads, fringes, caftans and sandals of the hippies.

Long hair would often have plaited strands with brightly coloured braids woven through and beads or feathers attached at the ends.

His brightly coloured and patterned clothes would have been unthought of a few years earlier. His long hair is tied back by a band, hippie-style; the pink shades perched on his nose are purely a fashion accessory. A more hippie look could be achieved by letting him carry a beaded and fringed shoulder bag.

A denim hotpants suit was an alternative to the mini-skirt. Tights would have been worn under it in colder weather.

His jeans are the epitome of the 1970s, tight over the hips and thighs and widely flared at the bottom.

Heavy, clog-type shoes with platform soles were designed to show off slim ankles.

Platform shoes with high heels were worn by both sexes.

PANTOMIME AND MUSICALS

The skirt of this milkmaid costume is given shape and bounce with layers of frilled petticoats.

PANTOMIMES ARE BASED ON CHILDREN'S STORIES SUCH AS *SLEEPING BEAUTY* AND ARE PERFORMED OVER THE CHRISTMAS PERIOD. MUSICALS AND OPERETTAS ARE STYLED ACCORDING TO THE TIME IN WHICH THEY ARE SET: E.G. *CAMELOT* IS COSTUMED IN MEDIEVAL STYLE, AND *GUYS AND DOLLS* IN 1930S' DRESS.

Making costumes for musicals and pantomimes can be great fun. Costumes are more exaggerated than in other plays and the design and colour should have a greater visual impact.

PANTOMIME

When dressing pantomime characters there are two very basic rules to remember: the first is to exaggerate the difference between rich and poor; the second to exaggerate the style and decoration of the costumes. Colour and the use of different fabrics will help achieve both these objectives.

Pantomime tradition demands that certain female roles are played by men and certain male roles by women. In *Cinderella*, for example, the parts of the Ugly Sisters are usually played by men, that of the Prince by a woman. The men are referred to as pantomime dames; the women as principal boys. You may also have to make costumes for various comic animals, such as a horse, a cow, a cat or a hen.

MUSICALS

A musical, like a play, has leading roles, but unlike a play it has a chorus line – a group of artistes that are the mainstay of the big song and dance routines. Leotards can be used as the base for many modern styles of costume. They can be appliquéed with material and lace, embroidered with beads and sequins, and worn under full-circle skirts.

Costumes must not restrict the movements of any of the artistes. Singers do not like costumes with restricting necklines. Female dancers' waists need to be free of belts and any decoration that could impede the lifts performed by their male dancing partners.

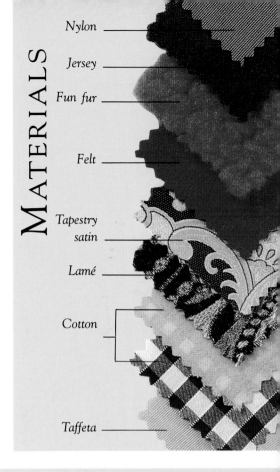

MATERIALS

Nylon
Jersey
Fun fur
Felt
Tapestry satin
Lamé
Cotton
Taffeta

ACCESSORIES

Thread together beads and scarabs to make an Egyptian neckpiece.

A papier mâché serpant's head attached to a circlet makes an Egyptian headpiece.

Animal heads are essential for pantomimes. Use wire and papier mache covered with fake fur and felt.

Red satin pumps can be used for Snow White and Dorothy in The Wizard of Oz.

PANTOMIME DAME

USE LARGE, BRIGHTLY COLOURED CLOTHES WHICH SHOULD BE DECORATED GARISHLY. THERE ARE VARIOUS METHODS OF MAKING PADDING, FROM STUFFING BRAS TO CREATING A STUFFED BODICE.

To pad a bodice, fit it on a tailor's dummy and pad out with layers of wadding as required. Hold the wadding in place with strips of fabric cut on the cross. Use this method to create big bottoms and stomachs, giant shoulders and hump backs.

The most versatile method of padding is to make a long fitted bodice, in flesh-coloured transparent nylon if it will be seen or cotton if it will not. It should finish at the top of the legs and fasten at the centre back with tapes. This can then have padding attached as required.

A very large bra can be stuffed with cotton wool. Sew fabric over to hold the cotton wool in place.

Use hip pads to exaggerate the actor's bottom.

As a quick improvisation sew tapes to a large square feather cushion and secure it round the body.

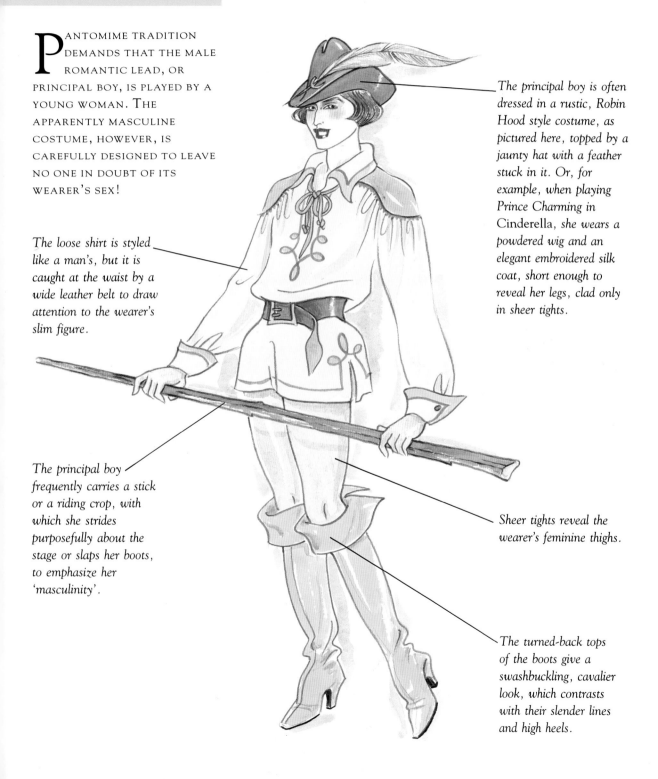

PERIOD COSTUMES

PRINCIPAL BOY

PANTOMIME TRADITION DEMANDS THAT THE MALE ROMANTIC LEAD, OR PRINCIPAL BOY, IS PLAYED BY A YOUNG WOMAN. THE APPARENTLY MASCULINE COSTUME, HOWEVER, IS CAREFULLY DESIGNED TO LEAVE NO ONE IN DOUBT OF ITS WEARER'S SEX!

The loose shirt is styled like a man's, but it is caught at the waist by a wide leather belt to draw attention to the wearer's slim figure.

The principal boy frequently carries a stick or a riding crop, with which she strides purposefully about the stage or slaps her boots, to emphasize her 'masculinity'.

The principal boy is often dressed in a rustic, Robin Hood style costume, as pictured here, topped by a jaunty hat with a feather stuck in it. Or, for example, when playing Prince Charming in Cinderella, she wears a powdered wig and an elegant embroidered silk coat, short enough to reveal her legs, clad only in sheer tights.

Sheer tights reveal the wearer's feminine thighs.

The turned-back tops of the boots give a swashbuckling, cavalier look, which contrasts with their slender lines and high heels.

STAGE CAT

ALONG SLEEVED, HIGH-NECKED BLACK LEOTARD AND TIGHTS FORM THE BASIS OF A GOOD CAT COSTUME. ALTERNATIVELY, YOU COULD IMPROVISE WITH A SHORT, FUR FABRIC COAT. MAKE A TAIL FROM FUR FABRIC IN A SIMILAR WAY TO THE PANTOMIME COW'S TAIL.

An eye mask made from black fabric with almond shaped cut-outs for the eyes can be worn in addition to make-up.

A balaclava or pull-on ski mask, with fur fabric ears sewn on, can be used to create the head, and the face painted on with make-up.

Patches of felt can be sewn onto the leotard for decoration.

An alternative head can be made using a soft toy pattern, scaling the head up to the size you need. Make eyelashes from strips of felt cut into a fringe, and whiskers from pipe cleaners.

A hen costume is constructed in the same way as that of a cat, using a brown leotard and yellow or red tights. Feathers are used to make the tail, and red felt to make the head combs.

Plain black ballet pumps should be used.

PERIOD COSTUMES

PANTOMIME COW

ANY FOUR-LEGGED ANIMAL CAN BE MADE EASILY FROM TWO PAIRS OF BAGGY TROUSERS FOR THE LEGS, A RECTANGLE THROW-OVER FOR THE BODY AND A HEAD MOULDED FROM PAPIER MÂCHÉ. USE TWO CONTRASTING COLOURS OF JERSEY FABRIC.

Glue strands of wool between the ears to form a fringe and make horns from cardboard or papier mâché.

Make the head from papier mâché, moulding it onto a framework of chicken wire. Make sure the cut ends of the wire are turned in so they cannot injure the wearer. Remember to leave openings in the head for the front person to see through – usually through the head's eyes, but sometimes through its mouth.

Make a tail from a tube of fabric with a fringe at the bottom or use plaited wool with one end left loose.

Make a throw-over for the body. It needs to be long enough to completely cover the two people inside, lengthways and widthways, bearing in mind that the front person stands and the back one crouches. Leave an opening for the head.

Cut large, mis-shaped pieces from a different coloured fabric and sew them at random on the throw-over and legs.

UNIFORMS

The Roman soldier's upper torso was protected by a breastplate. The skirt is made from rectangles of leather.

PRODUCTIONS WHICH FEATURE UNIFORMS INCLUDE *CYRANO DE BERGERAC* AND GILBERT AND SULLIVAN'S OPERETTA, *HMS PINAFORE*. UNIFORMS GENERALLY REFLECT THE PERIOD IN WHICH THE PLAY IS SET. HERE WE CONCENTRATE ON FOUR STYLES: MEDIEVAL, SIXTEENTH CENTURY, SEVENTEENTH CENTURY AND NINETEENTH CENTURY.

When designing a uniform it is important to remember what the wearing of it represents. It identifies the wearer as a member of a particular group of people, whether that be a school or an army. In battle it is important in recognizing opposing forces. Colour plays an important role in distinguishing both officers and regiments; emblems and insignia, dating back hundreds of years, are still worn today. In modern times, however, a similarity has come about in uniforms throughout the world for reasons of practicality, and it is harder to distinguish between opposing forces. Often the main distinction is in the headdress. In the past helmets were important badges of recognition, their shape and adornment distinguishing opposing forces, regiments within those forces, and officers from men.

The box pleat style of the pockets of this WWII army jacket is still in use today. The epaulettes are made of the jacket fabric and are less decorative than those on earlier uniforms.

MATERIALS

Felt

Wool

Tweed wool

Wool facecloth

Leather

ACCESSORIES

Leather gaiters can be copied using vinyl material.

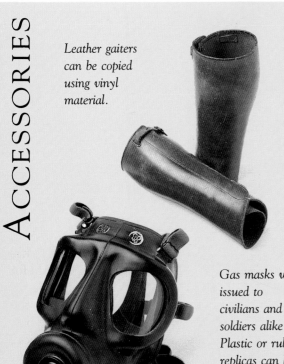

Cover cardboard with fabric and attach fringes to the outer curve to make epaulettes.

Gas masks were issued to civilians and soldiers alike. Plastic or rubber replicas can be bought in toy shops.

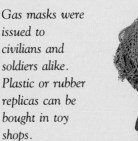

Trench helmets can be bought or you can cover a hard hat with khaki netting.

Yᴏᴜ ᴡɪʟʟ ɴᴇᴇᴅ ᴀ ꜱʟᴇᴇᴠᴇʟᴇꜱꜱ, ᴄʀᴏᴛᴄʜ-ʟᴇɴɢᴛʜ ᴜɴᴅᴇʀᴛᴜɴɪᴄ ɪɴ ʀᴏᴜɢʜ ɢʀᴇʏ ᴛᴡᴇᴇᴅ ᴏʀ ᴡᴏᴏʟ, ᴄʜᴀɪɴ ᴍᴀɪʟ ꜰᴏʀ ᴛʜᴇ ʟᴇɢꜱ, ᴀʀᴍꜱ ᴀɴᴅ ʜᴇᴀᴅ, ᴀɴᴅ ᴀ ᴛᴀʙᴀʀᴅ. Yᴏᴜ ᴍᴀʏ ᴀʟꜱᴏ ɴᴇᴇᴅ ᴀ ʜᴇʟᴍᴇᴛ, ꜱᴡᴏʀᴅ ᴀɴᴅ ꜱʜɪᴇʟᴅ.

Shape a helmet from chicken wire, cover it in polythene, then with papier mâché. The polythene enables you to remove the papier mâché from the wire when it is dry. You could also improvise a helmet from cardboard or an old felt hat, cut to shape and painted silver.

Make a chain-mail balaclava (use a knitting pattern) and paint it metallic silver.

Decorate the tabard with an heraldic symbol or a Crusader's red cross cut out of felt and sewn or appliquéed in place.

Make a shield from stiff cardboard and paint it silver. Decorate the front with an heraldic symbol or cross. Attach loops of tape at the back of the shield through which the arm can be slipped to carry it.

A wide leather belt is worn over the tabard.

Make a sword from stiff cardboard or wood. Paint it silver and decorate the cross-piece of the handle.

Knit chain mail in brown string or wool using a plain knit stitch. Panel shapes fit over the arms and legs and can be sprayed with silver paint. Hand-sew the sleeves to the undertunic and attach the legs with tapes.

Fit cork insoles both inside and outside the feet of the chain mail to prevent the actor slipping on stage.

PERIOD COSTUMES

16TH CENTURY

ARCHERS AND FOOT SOLDIERS WORE PADDED, CROTCH-LENGTH TUNICS UNDER LEATHER JERKINS, LOOSE KNEE BREECHES AND BOOTS. NOBLEMEN AND OFFICERS WORE DOUBLETS, USUALLY PADDED, UNDER METAL BREASTPLATES, PUFFED KNEE BREECHES, STOCKINGS AND LEATHER BOOTS.

A short, circular cloak can be tied over the back and wings added to the shoulders of the doublet.

Here, a full-sleeved shirt is worn directly beneath a sleeveless doublet. A breastplate is worn on top.

A leather jerkin for an archer or foot soldier can be made like the Elizabethan man's jacket, minus the sleeves. The front should be fastened with leather lacing.

Mould the breastplate with thick felt or cardboard round a tailor's dummy, wetting it and pressing it to the right shape. Leave it to dry and stiffen. You can also make papier mâché armour in this way. Sew or staple tapes at the shoulders and sides of the breastplate for tying it in place.

Use the helmet from the medieval uniform.

Officers would also carry muskets. Spurs can be worn at the heels.

18TH CENTURY

USE THE SHORT FITTED BODICE WITH LONG FRONT AND BACK PANELS TO MAKE A COAT. ADD POCKET FLAPS. YOU WILL ALSO NEED A FULL-SLEEVED SHIRT, A CROTCH-LENGTH WAISTCOAT AND A CRAVAT.

Make crossbelts out of stiff white tape, and add a wide leather belt, from which the sword is slung, usually on the left side. Pouches were worn at the back of the belt containing powder and shot.

Cut stiff felt or cardboard epaulettes to shape, glue fabric on one side and upholstery fringe round the curved ends if required. Attach the epaulettes to the shoulders of the coat with large buttons.

Strips of braid can be used to decorate the cuffs, pocket flaps and collar. Wider strips can be attached to the centre front of the coat with buttons. Alternatively, the coat can be cut double breasted and have contrasting coloured facings attached.

The coat skirts should be fastened back to reveal coloured facings.

Use leggings, with a pair of white leg warmers over the top on the lower legs, or calf-length black boots.

19TH CENTURY

THE BODY OF THE COAT IS MADE FROM THE SHORT FITTED BODICE. A BASQUE OR SKIRT CAN BE ADDED IF REQUIRED. THE COAT SHOULD BE BUTTONED FROM WAIST TO NECK AND HAVE A STIFF, STAND-UP COLLAR. ONLY OFFICERS CARRIED SWORDS.

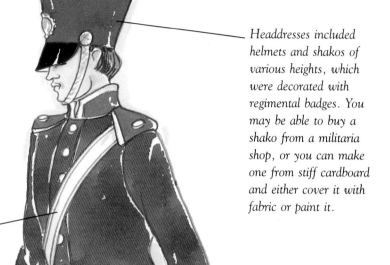

Headdresses included helmets and shakos of various heights, which were decorated with regimental badges. You may be able to buy a shako from a militaria shop, or you can make one from stiff cardboard and either cover it with fabric or paint it.

A single leather band should be worn as a sash; officers wore a fabric sash instead. A wide leather belt can be worn round the waist.

The collar, cuffs and epaulettes can be in a contrasting colour, and decorated with flat braid. Epaulettes may be shaped or straight.

Adapt modern tapered trousers by sewing flat wool or silk braid stripes down the outside seams.

TRICKS OF THE TRADE

BAGGING OUT

Tailored garments are extremely difficult to make. A simple method which can be used is called "bagging out".

ONE

Cut out all of the pattern pieces in both outer and lining fabrics. Tack the main body of the outer garment together and fit the garment on the wearer. Make alterations as necessary. The centre back seam of jackets should then be machined. Machine the centre back seam of the lining pieces together also. Make up sleeves separately at the end.

PROFESSIONAL COSTUMIERS EMPLOY MANY DIFFERENT TRICKS AND SHORTCUTS TO MAKE THEIR COSTUMES ADAPTABLE, QUICK AND EASY TO MAKE, AND COST EFFECTIVE. MANY OF THESE WILL BE ESPECIALLY USEFUL TO AMATEUR DRAMATIC GROUPS WHO GENERALLY HAVE LIMITED TIME, MONEY AND EXPERIENCE.

FOUR

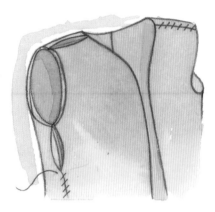

Turn the material right side out through the unattached edges and press the edges flat where the outer and lining fabrics have been joined – this is the "bagging out" process. Next, sew the remaining seams of the garment together, only taking in the back piece of the lining fabric for each section. Press the seams flat in one direction and then slipstitch the unattached front lining piece in place to encase the seams neatly.

TWO

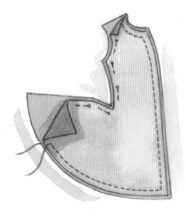

Pin the lining pieces to the corresponding outer fabric pieces, right sides together. Work out which edges of the garment will not be joined to any other pattern piece and machine these seams only.

THREE

For example, a Restoration coat will have the neck, front edges, hem and skirt edges machined; only the side seams and shoulder seams would not be stitched at this stage.

FIVE

Sleeves are attached to their lining pieces at the hems. When sewing the sleeves into the main body of the garment, the sleeve lining is left unattached and then slipstitched neatly in place as described in step four.

ALTERING THE SIZE

Wherever possible, make allowances for adjusting the size of garments at a later stage. This makes costumes useable by different-sized people and may also be necessary if an actor loses or gains weight during rehearsals.

ONE

Always leave extra elastic in waistbands, cuffs, etc and, wherever possible, leave a wide hem allowance for letting down at a later date.

TWO

Allow extra material in seams if possible. If the seam is to be bound, it is useful to attach the binding before sewing the seam. This enables you to alter the garment to fit others without taking off the binding and without the need to find extra fabric for rebinding.

TEMPLATES

Templates are used as patterns for cutting a garment and also to create decorative edgings.

ONE

Use old items of clothing as pattern templates. Take them apart at the seams and copy the basic shapes.

TWO

Dagged and scalloped edges are easy to do. Design your template and cut it out in cardboard. On the wrong side of the fabric, draw round the template along the edge which is to be decorated, leaving a small seam allowance. Pin lining or facing material onto the outer fabric, right sides together. Sew along the lines you have drawn with the template. Cut the material to shape and then notch the seam allowance. Turn right side out and press the edges flat. Slipstitch the unattached edge of the facing to hold it in position.

REPLICA COSTUMES

Replica costumes are sometimes needed, usually to denote the passing of time. These replicas must therefore look more worn.

ONE

Break down the garment with paint or a cheese grater to age it. Always do this unevenly to produce a more natural effect.

TWO

The problem of "blood" on costumes can be solved by attaching false fronts with velcro, removing them and washing them – most stage blood will wash out. Or try to dress the character in a washable shirt or bodice when the blood is to be used, and keep a duplicate shirt or bodice available for the next performance to allow the soiled one to be laundered.

SLASHES

There are quite a few techniques you can use to imitate slashes and improve their appearance.

ONE

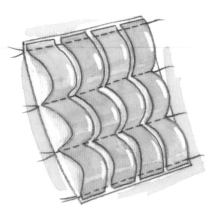

Cut strips of material to length and width required or use lengths of wide ribbon. Sew them to the garment at the top and bottom edges, leaving the sides loose so that the material of the undergarment shows through to give a slashed effect. The strips can also be attached along their length at intervals to give a looped effect.

TWO

If the undergarment is never going to be exposed and serves no other purpose than to be seen through slashes, it can be omitted and strips of material sewn behind the slashes instead. These should be pulled through slightly and then tacked in place.

CUTTING ON THE CROSS

Fabric cut on the cross is more elastic and is used for binding edges and to make garments which must fit tightly.

ONE

Lay the fabric flat with the selvage against a straight edge and cut your material diagonally across it. A bodice cut on the cross will mould itself to the wearer.

TWO

When binding edges, if one strip is not long enough, cut several and stitch them together as shown. To attach the binding, place the fabrics right sides together, matching the raw edges, and machine. Turn the binding to the wrong side, fold in the raw edge and hem by hand, attaching it on the inside to the line of machine stitching.

MATERIALS

Fabrics come in all sorts of widths and you will often have to make adjustments to accommodate this.

ONE

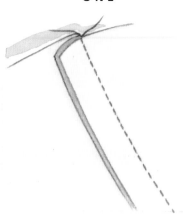

If the fabric you want to use is not available in the width you need, sew an extra strip onto it before you start cutting out your garment.

TWO

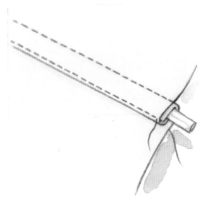

If you run out of cotton tape to use as channelling when boning a petticoat, you can make a channel by folding the garment at the position where you wish the bone to go and measuring from the fold the width needed for the bone. Machine at this level all round, leaving an opening for the bone to slot through. Press the channel down one way so it lies flat, and machine along the edge of the fold to anchor the channel in place.

THREE

If you cannot get any plastic bones, don't be afraid to improvise. You can use many of the modern plastic-coated wires found around the house or garden. Always take care to cover the ends of wires with sticky tape to stop them injuring the wearer.

PIPING

Finishing edges with a length of piping enables the various elements of a costume to be finished separately and then joined through the piping as necessary.

ONE

Cut a crossway strip of fabric approximately 8cm (3in) wide and a little longer than the seam you are going to attach it to. Encase the piping cord on the wrong side of the material. Machine or hand sew tightly against the cord.

TWO

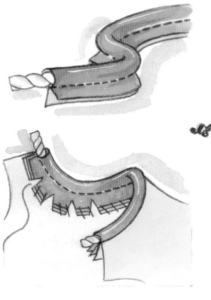

Place the encased cord on the hem you wish to pipe on the right side of the fabric and machine it in place close to the cord. Make a finished edge by stitching the bias into a hem. Necklines, especially square ones, should be finished in this way.

FASTENERS

For quick changes, it is essential to choose the type of fasteners for a garment carefully and to position them in the most convenient place.

ONE

It is often easier on skirts and trousers to have openings on the side seams, fastened with either a zip, velcro or a placket with hooks and bars. Disguise zips on the centre back of dresses with small pearl buttons sewn on one side of the opening.

TWO

Lacing is time-consuming and should be avoided wherever possible. Mock lacing can be attached by sewing flat loops of tape where the opening is supposed to be and then threading a cord from bottom to top in a crosswise manner. Mock lacing is also a useful way of making the size of a garment adjustable.

INDEX

CREDITS

Quarto would like to acknowledge and thank Academy Costumes
Limited, London, and the Royal National Theatre, London, for
providing costumes and accessories used in photography.

We would also like to thank Donald Cooper at Photostage for kindly
allowing us to reproduce the photographs of stage productions shown
on pages 7, 14, 30, 36, 40, 48 and 60.